Flags in the Window

Studies in the Postmodern Theory of Education

Joe L. Kincheloe and Shirley R. Steinberg
General Editors

Vol. 314

PETER LANG
New York • Washington, D.C./Baltimore • Bern
Frankfurt am Main • Berlin • Brussels • Vienna • Oxford

Norman K. Denzin

Flags in the Window

Dispatches from the American War Zone

PETER LANG
New York • Washington, D.C./Baltimore • Bern
Frankfurt am Main • Berlin • Brussels • Vienna • Oxford

Library of Congress Cataloging-in-Publication Data

Denzin, Norman K.
Flags in the window: dispatches from the American war zone /
Norman K. Denzin.
p. cm.
Includes bibliographical references and index.
1. Political culture—United States. 2. Democracy—United States.
3. Patriotism—United States. 4. National characteristics, American.
5. September 11 Terrorist Attacks, 2001—Influence. 6. Iraq War, 2003-.
7. Presidents—United States—Election—2004. 8. United States—Politics
and government—2001-. 9. United States—Foreign relations—2001-.
I. Series: Counterpoints: studies in the postmodern
theory of education, 1058-1634; v. 314.
E902 .D465 973.931 22 2007003224
ISBN 978-1-4331-0034-5 (hard cover)
ISBN 978-0-8204-8818-9 (paperback)
ISSN 1058-1634

Bibliographic information published by **Die Deutsche Bibliothek**.
Die Deutsche Bibliothek lists this publication in the "Deutsche
Nationalbibliografie"; detailed bibliographic data is available
on the Internet at http://dnb.ddb.de/.

Cover design by Lisa Barfield

29 Broadway, 18th floor, New York, NY 10006
www.peterlang.com

Contents

Preface

Written over a four year period, originally conceived as "Notes from a Homeland War Diary", these short essays—record on-going reactions—reports from the war zone—to what Joan Didion calls the "new normal" under the Bush Administration. They rethink questions of power, political authority, patriotism, democracy, science, civil society, and the academy.

Acknowledgments

I would like to thank Chris Myers, Shirley Steinberg, and Joe Kincheloe for their quick and early support of this project. I wish thank Bernadette Shade, production manager at Peter Lang, for shepherding this book through all phases of production, Christina Ceisel for her assistance in the copyediting process, James Salvo for assistance in every way possible, Jack Bratich, Michael Giardina, and Katherine Ryan for on-going conversations on life in the new normal.

Earlier portions of the materials in Chapter One appeared in Norman K. Denzin, 2002, "Critical Inquiry in America After 11 September 2001." *Cultural Studies—Critical Methodologies*, 2, 1, pp. 5–8; earlier portions of the material in Chapter Two appeared in Norman K. Denzin, 2002, "What Will we Tell the Children?" *Cultural-Studies—Critical Methodologies*, 2, 20, pp. 214–216; earlier portions of the material in Chapter Three appeared in Norman K. Denzin, 2002, "Week Four, A New War," *Qualitative Inquiry*, 8, 2, pp. 199–202; earlier portions of Chapter Seven, appeared in Norman K. Denzin, 2004, "The War on Culture, the War on Truth, Part 1," *Cultural Studies—Critical Methodologies*, 5, 1, 126–131; earlier portions of Chapter Ten appeared in Norman K. Denzin, 2005, "Homegrown democracy, Homegrown Democrats," *Cultural Studies—Critical Methodologies*, 5, 1, pp. 126–131; an alternative version of Chapter 12 will appear in Norman K. Denzin, 2007, "Science Under Bush," *Qualitative*

Inquiry. 13; an abbreviated version of Chapter 13 appeared in Norman K. Denzin, "Katrina and the Collapse of Civil Society in New Orleans," *Space and Culture: International Journal of Social Spaces*, 9, 1, pp. 95–99; an abbreviated version of Chapter 14 will appear in Norman K. Denzin, "The Secret Downing Street Memo and the Politics of Truth," *Cultural Studies—Critical Methodologies*, 6.

Part 1

9-11-01–10-30-01

1

"Critical Inquiry in America after 11 September 2001"

(9-24-01)[1]

The world changed on 11 September 2001. The attacks on the World Trade Center in New York City and the Pentagon in Washington, D. C. produced a horror, to quote New York City Mayor Rudolph W. Giuliani, that is more than the mind can bear. Confused, angry, depressed, full of grief, not knowing how to act, Americans watched their TV screens and read their newspapers, seeking direction from those who would bring meaning to this event.

This moment requires critically informed responses from the academy. Such responses will help people recover meaning in the face of this senseless, brutal violence; a violence that continues to produce voiceless screams of terror and insanity; a violence and a horror punctuated by stories certain to become part of urban folklore. A young child awakens her mother, "Mommy can we use the cellphone to call Daddy in heaven?" (Tierney, 2001, p. A24).

Policing the Crisis

Stealing a title from Stuart Hall et al. (1978), it is necessary to police the present international crisis, to create a critical dialogue focused on history and politics as they unfold in front of us. The starting point for this dialogue is painful.

1. Date the essay was written.

Jonathan Schell is correct, "*There is no technical solution to the vulnerability of modern populations to weapons of mass destruction*" (Schell, 2001, p. 5, italics in original). Terrorism may be abetted, but it cannot be stopped. No amount of money, no stealth system, no security system will stop violence. To think otherwise is to participate in an escalating self-destructive process that is guaranteed to produce destruction on a world-wide basis.

Starting with this fact, the dialogue must move in at least three directions at the same time. First, we must start with the personal and the biographical, the human tragedies following 11 September, and each person's intersection with this event. We need a critical, humane discourse that creates sacred and spiritual spaces for persons and their moral communities, spaces where people can express and give meaning to the tragedy and its aftermath. This project will work back and forth, connecting the personal, the political, and the cultural.

Second, a critical discourse must be launched at the level of the media and the ideological, including discourses on war, America, democracy, and the silences surrounding peace, human rights, and non-violence. This discourse will call for justice without war. It will ask for calm deliberations. It will plead against rash actions which could erode human rights and civil liberties. It will ask, "Whose democracy?" Whose America?"

We do not have a strong, independent, critical press in America (McChesney, 2000, p. x). We have a media which can instantly produce a sea of violent images, a media with a memory, but no critical history (Baudrillard, 1988, p. 126). Mainstream media have more or less uncritically adopted President Bush's rhetoric: We are at war; this is our Pearl Harbor; we were attacked by cowards; America's freedoms are under assault; an international war on terrorists and terrorism must be launched; if innocent citizens are killed, so be it.

The narrative is straight forward. Benign global techno-capitalism and the values of a free democratic world were attacked on dark Tuesday. Working from this premise, acting under the umbrella of an increasingly conservative, right-wing neo-liberal agenda, President Bush and his National Security Advisers have moved quickly and decisively. The mythology of the Wild West is operative: " Osama bin Laden, Dead or Alive."

The "Dead or Alive" political logic works thusly: "Because America is a democracy . . . some democratic perquisites might have to be abandoned. What might this mean? Increased domestic snooping by US law enforcement and intelligence agencies, ethnic profiling, another drive for a national ID card system" (Cockburn, 2001, p. 8). Congress promises to bail out the greedy airline industry. The lid is off Social Security. Over thirty-five thousand national guard troops have been put on alert. Repressive, global corporate politics drive internal domestic policies.

The moral conservatives blame the event on homosexuals and the women's movement. The political conservatives say we have gone soft on national defense. The transition to a reactionary neo-fascist state is sped up. State-sponsored violence is a taken for granted. The boundaries of personal democratic freedom are shrinking. The very foundations of our democratic institutions are under assault. And it all happened, it seems, in one week.

Third, we need a critical national conversation on what is happening, a coalition of voices across the political, cultural and religious spectrums, the socialist left, the green, peace, women's, gay, lesbian, African and Asian-American, Latinio, movements; libertarians, young, old, students, workers, the clergy and persons from all religions, intellectuals. Every era must develop its own theory of radical politics and social democracy; so must ours (see Kellner, 1989, p. 227).

We must be vigilant against the forces of fascism and state-sponsored violence, and surveillance done in the name of freedom. We must question flag-waving, "Whose flag is being waved, and what does it mean?" We cannot let democratic dialogue be eviscerated in a time of crisis. We cannot allow attacks on persons of color. We cannot let the political discourse be shaped by the needs and voices of multinational corporations (Giroux, 2000a, p. 13; 2000b, p. 15). We must ask "Who is guarding our freedom?" and "What did America do to provoke this violence?"

These and other questions are raised in the commentary which follows. Readers are invited to enter into a conversation about a practical, progressive politics, a radical discourse linking "ethics, politics, and power" (Giroux, 2000b p. 25). America and cultural studies are indeed at a crossroads. The need to be radical, utopian and humane has never been greater. We demand a road map for the future, a democractic performative cultural studies that shows us how to do this.

Coda

There were powerful glimpses of hope and humanity underneath the violent images that circulated in the media during the week of September 11. A sea of photographs on walls and fences, pictures of human beings lost in the tragedy. Behind the faces pasted on hand-held posters there was a sense that we were a nation of people who felt deeply. Each photograph reached back to a tiny island of humanity, mothers, fathers, friends and co-workers, ordinary people who would never return a home. A three year-old asking her mother to call daddy in heaven. Beneath the flags and the tears, there was a heartfelt emotion, a love and a humanity that transcended the horror of it all.

References

Baudrillard, Jean. (1988). *America*. London: Verso.

Cockburn, Alexander. (2001). "Faceless Cowards?." *The Nation* 1 October; 8.

Giroux, Henry. (2000a). *Impure Acts: The Practical Politics of Cultural Studies*. New York: Routledge.

Giroux, Henry. (2000b). *Stealing Innocence: Corporate Culture's War on Children*. New York: Palgrave.

Hall, Stuart, et al. (1978). *Policing the Crisis: Mugging the State, and Law and Order*. New York: Holmes and Meier.

Kellner, Douglas. (1989). *Critical Theory, Marxism and Modernity*. Baltimore: Johns Hopkins University Press.

McChesney, Robert W. (2000). *Rich Media, Poor Democracy*. Urbana: University of Illinois Press.

Nelson, Cary, and Dilip Parameshwar. (1996). Cultural studies and the Politics of Disciplinarity. In C. Nelson and D. Parameshwar (Eds.), *Displinarity and Dissent in Cultural Studies* (pp 1–19). New York: Routledge.

Schnell, Jonathan. (2001). "A Hole in the world." *The Nation*, 1 October, 4–6.

Tierney, John. (2001, September 18). "Fantasies of Vengeance Fed by Fury." *The New York Times*, p. A24.

2

What Will We Tell the Children?

(11-10-01)

Writing two days after 11 September 2001, upon first hearing of the airplanes and the towers, Laurel Richardson (2002, pp. 23) asked, "What will the children be told?

She answered her own question,

> "And then I see that the children are being told, as the adults are, through television cameras and media voices. The children are seeing the airplane and the second tower, and the airplane/tower, airplane/tower over and over until it's All Fall Down. And All Fall Down again and again."

The next day she called her grandson's mother who reported that he was afraid an airplane would hit his school.

What will we tell the children?

What can we tell our children when we all being told the same thing they are? Do we tell our daughters and sons that if you challenge the pictures and the stories on TV you are betraying President Bush? Do we tell our grandchildren that those who raise doubts may be traitors? Do we tell them that peace protesters are challenging President Bush and threatening America's mission in this war, a war that is still unofficial? Do we say that it is unpatriotic to seek the goals of peace and justice? Do we teach them that in a democracy there can be no dissent? What if they answer that a genuine democracy requires opposition and criticism? Must we remain silent?

On 12 September, writing from New York City, Michelle Fine (2002, pp. 138–139) reported that

> You can tell who's dead or missing by their smiles. Their photos dot the subways, ferries, trains and Port Authority Terminal, shockingly alive with joy, comfort and pleasure. They died before they could know what we now know. The not-dead travel on subways and trains filled with hollow eyes; no smiles; shoulders down. Now a flood of flags, talk of God, military and patriotism chase us all.

What will we tell the children?

What will we tell the mothers, the fathers, the wives and husbands, those with hollow eyes, no smiles. Yesterday a New York City widow killed herself. Her husband died on 11 September.

Yvonna S. Lincoln (2002) speaks for those for whom the expression of grief does not come easily. For persons, like herself raised to hide their sorrow, "The end result, I have come to realize, is a human being who lives with his or her grief for all their days. The future, like tears, never comes.

What will we tell the children?

Do we allow our children to grieve? What are they grieving for? What are we grieving for? I'm grieving for a lost democracy. So what does grief mean in a time like this? For whom and for what are we grieving?

* * * * * *

Two days ago the *New York Times* ran a picture of an Afghanistan mother and her ten day-old daughter huddled under a blanket in an earthen cave outside Kandahar. Bomb craters surrounded the earthen structure. Mountain peaks hovered in the distance. A clear-white jet trail cut the vivid blue sky in half, as a U. S. bomber returned to base. What will this mother tell her daughter, if they get out of this mess alive? Will she tell her that the Americans came to Afghanistan to free women from the Taliban? Or will she say that the Americans with their planes and their bombs are on a mission to destroy terrorism?

The earth is a living thing. Of course we all know this. The earth is more than a set of coordinates on a map, it is more than a physically bounded geographical site. The earth is a living thing. The earth and its places ought not be transformed into bomb sites. When we allow language to do this, we turn people into military targets. The earth and the people who make up the country called Afghanistan have been turned into targets for America's war machine. They are already dead, even before the bombs hit the ground.

* * * * *

Invoking and paraphrasing William Kittridge (1987, p. 87) in America today, in the brutally cruel cold days since 11 September we are struggling to revise our dominant mythology. Just who are we as Americans? What story about ourselves do we want to inhabit? Who are our storytellers, whose stories will we accept? Which laws will we allow to control our lives?

We want laws designed to preserve a model of a radically peaceful democratic society, a society which is non-violent. We want laws and courts based on a post-11 September mythology. We want a new mythology for America. We must re-imagine our myths. Only then can we coherently remodel our laws, and hope to keep our society in a realistic relationship to our utopian democratic ideals. Then we will know what to tell the children.

References

Fine, Michelle. (2002). The Mourning After. *Qualitative Inquiry*, 8; 137–148.

Kittridge, William. (1987). *Owning It All*. San Francisco: Murray House.

Lincoln, Yvonna S. (2002). Grief in an Appalachian Register. *Qualitative Inquiry*, 8; in press.

Richardson, Laurel. 2002. "Small World." *Cultural Studies—Critical Methodologies*, 2(1): 23–25.

3

Week Four, a New War

(11-5-01)

Week Four of the War

Newspaper headlines: U. S. planes bomb Taliban artillery near a rebel artery. Mr. Rumsfeld cautions that rooting out terrorism is a difficult task that will take time and patience. Coordination between American air strikes and the battlefield remains problematic. Twice in two days American bombs were dropped on Red Cross headquarters. Efforts to calm the nation's fears over the anthrax threat spin out of control. We are days away from Ramadan, Islam's sacred month of fasting. But wars rarely pause for holy days. Secretary Rumsfeld informs us that Muslim nations have often made war on one another during Ramadan. Does God take sides?

* * * * * * * * * * *

The war goes on. Bahawalpur, Pakistan. October 28

At 8: 50 a. m. on this bright sunny autumn Sunday morning "three young men with Kalashnikolv rifles walked into St. Dominic's Roman Catholic Church

. . . A group of 35 Pakistani Protestants. . . . were just preparing to go home. . . . the intruders opened fire . . . Blood everywhere" (Burns, 2001, p. A1). Sixteen people died.

The theory, uncontested, shared by Christians, Muslim clerics, and Hindu sadhus was that the killers "were acting to avenge the American bombing of Afghanistan. 'The Americans are attacking Afghanistan, and we are Christians, and America is mostly a Christian country, and so it is a matter of revenge,' said Elizabeth David, a nurse at the railway hospital" (Burns, 2001, p. A1). Her husband, an engineer, elaborated, "The trouble started when President Bush called America's war on terrorism a crusade . . . that means the revival of history . . . East against West, Islam against Christianity, and in Pakistan it means Muslims against Christians . . . and that means jihad" (Burns, 2001, B5).

* * * * * * * * * * *

Week Four. The War goes on.

"America on Alert." The F. B.I. has arrested 900 suspects, exactly zero have been criminally charged. It took the Bush Administration at least a week to realize that a second attack on America was underway. Following Administration directives, the major networks now censor the news about the war. A growing peace movement taking shape across America is ignored by the media. Patriotism is the national watch word. The American flag waves everywhere.

* * * * * * * * * * *

Game Two, World Series.

Last night in Phoenix, Arizona, Ray Charles sang the American Anthem. His piano was on the baseball field, which was covered by a huge American flag. High above the stadium the Stars and Stripes waved in the wind. Last night Ray Charles sang the "National Anthem" as only he can sing the blues. It was slow, and painful, drawn out, like a funeral dirge, like "St. James Infirmary." He wailed in the high notes, his voice full of sorrow, and suffering. It was as if he felt the blues for America, as if he was singing at America's funeral. And in that moment I was taken back to June Jordan's jazz prose poem, "Good News' Blues," a poem written about Billie Holiday and her version of the blues:

In Billie's land
It's never mind
about the prosecutors
and the INS
and the po-lice politicians . . .
and never mind
Apache helicopters
carrying a war load
cost more than it cost to build
2 hospitals
4 schools (Jordan, 1998, p. 194).

No "Good News Blues" in America today.

* * * * * * * * * * *

Annie Dillard says that divinity is not playful, that the universe was not made in jest, but in "solemn incomprehensible earnest. By a power that is unfathomably secret, and holy and fleet" (1974, p. 270), and violent. I choose to believe this.

In the "Peace of Wild Things" Wendell Berry (1998, p. 30) says that when

Despair for the world grows in me . . .
I go and lie down where the wood drake
rests in his beauty on the water, and the great heron feeds.
I come into the peace of wild things . . .
For a time I rest in the grace of the world, and am free.

* * * * * * * * * * *

Noon, 15 September: Mattis Lake, Champaign, Illinois

Fishing pole in hand, I parked and walked over a small hill to Mattis Lake, which is near my home. The lake is not large. It is surrounded by walking paths, and small picnic areas. An apartment complex hovers in the distance. Reeds, rushes and willows grow in its corners, and along its banks. Two tall maples shade the water where I stop. Rocks butt out into the water, bull rushes sway in the wind, grasshoppers sun themselves on blades of green grass, the noon sun dances off of the water, and waves ripple as the wind comes over the hill. I bait my hook with a dried up earthworm and cast my line into the water. Just as my red and white bobber settles on the surface, a tall sand crane makes a delicate landing on the grassy shoreline. As if on stilts, this elegantly awkward bird walks in an easterly direction, head darting back and forth, up and down, looking for I know not what.

My line is tugged sharply; I jerk my rod upward. A large bass jumps in the air. It jerks its head, and then dives down into deeper water. I set the hook and begin to reel in the line. The bass comes back to the surface, drawing near to the shore. I reach down and touch the fish, it must be over 12 inches long, and weigh over two pounds. I cradle the fish in my palm, holding it in the water I reach over with my other hand and remove the tiny hook from its jaw. I then put the fish back in the water and with a violent twist of its body, it disappears into the depths.

As I stand, to catch my breath, the sand crane, which has been watching me, flies off in haste, and on the distant shore ducks glide quietly into the hidden waters beneath a regal oak tree.

* * * * * * * * * *

In his anti-war anthem, Bob Dylan asks, "How many miles must a wild duck sail, before she sleeps in the sand?"

* * * * * * * * * *

In these times I seek the peace of wild things; wild ducks, sand cranes, geese flying south, and bass who swim in shallow waters. I accept a power that is unfathomably secret, and holy and fleet. But as part of the bargain I seek a serenity that allows me to rest in the grace of the world. I seek the self-awareness that will tell me when I must place myself in the presence of wild things. I want to live in a world where there are wild things who will tame my fears and my anger, wild things who do not tax their lives with grief and violence, wild things who do not have God on their side when they go to war.

* * * * * * * * * *

Acknowledgements: I thank Laurel Richardson and Yvonna S. Lincoln for their comments on earlier versions of this text.

References

Berry, Wendell. (1998). The Peace of Wild Things. In *The Selected Poems of Wendell Berry*, (p. 30). Washington, D. C.: Counterpoint.

Burns, John F. (2001, October 29) Gunmen Kill 16 Christians in Church in Pakistan. *New York Times*, pp. A1, B5.

Dillard, Annie. (1974). *Pilgrim at Tinker Creek*. New York: Harper & Row.

Jordan, June. (1998). "A Good News' Blues: A Jazz Prose-Poem." In June Jordan, *Affirmative Acts: Political Essays*, (pp. 182–200). New York: Doubleday.

Part 2

Iraq

4

Week 55: *Flags in the Window*

(12-3-02)

Week Fifty-Five of the War on Terrorism

America's on-ending war against terrorism is in its 55th week. We are starting our second year with Bush at war. In the first year of Bush's war Americans experienced considerable loss of personal freedom, witnessed major encroachments on civil rights, saw the President turn his back on the Kyoto Treaty, observed major corporate scandals starting with Enron, watched the Republicans take control of the House and Senate, as Bush bullied the United Nations into supporting the call for regime change in Iraq. During the first year of Bush's war, American foreign policy became more aggressive, with Bush claiming the right to attack any nation that might be a threat to America. America seems to be in a permanent war against the world.

In this fifty-fifth week newspaper headlines report such items as the following:

* Master of Secrets Leads a Tell-All Panel: Henry Kissinger to head a commission on September 11, 2001 attacks;
* Building up for the war in Iraq, the Pentagon converts unguided bombs into smart bombs;

* Congress allocates $133 million to buy 22 more Predators, which are aircraft used to track and kill people identified as Al Quaeda;
* Foot soldiers for the war in Iraq will be wired from head to foot with new combat kits which will include hand-held computers, and cords that run back to robotic vehicles;
* The pentagon launches a new satellite communications system using laser technology to transmit the huge amount of data gathered by foot soldiers;
* Francoise Dupros, communications director for the Canadian prime minister, is forced to resign after she said President Bush was a moron;
* Iraq admits inspectors;
* Bush administration rewrites environmental impact regulations including forest protection rules;
* Nearly every state is in a fiscal crisis, Bush administration says it cannot help;
* Tommy Ridge named first Secretary of Homeland Security.

* * * * * * * * * * *

18 September 2001 / 1 December 2002, Champaign, Illinois: Flags in the Window

Within a week of 9/11/01, in response to the terrorist attacks, flags, in all forms and sizes, began appearing in the windows of schools, private homes, automobiles, pick-ups, 18 wheelers, gas stations, K-Mart and Wal-Mart superstores, IGA grocery stores, clothing stores, shoe stores, book stores, and other public establishments. In Champaign, Illinois, the flags appeared in window after window of Central High School, the large public high school I ride by everyday on my bicycle on the way to campus.

In the weeks after 9/11/01, everywhere I looked, I saw flags of every type, size and shape: flag-pens, flag mousepads, flag-stickers, flags on poles that waved in the wind, flags on coffee cups, flags on radio antennas, big, little, and medium-sized flags. Flags so big they covered football fields. Songs about the flags became popular, songs with lines like, "Red, White and Blue, these colors don't run."

Last spring a woman in Urbana, Illinois made up a questionnaire and asked store-keepers why they had flags in their windows. "I was just curious," she replied, when asked why she had done this. Store owners reacted in anger and accused her of being a trouble-maker. People called the local talk radio station and wrote letters to the editor of our local paper. They said she was being unpatriotic.

* * * * * * * * * * *

Now it is Christmas time 2002, and the flags are still here. Flags have taken over Christmas. Flags have taken over Santa Claus and his reindeer and sled. At Market Place Mall, Santa's suit is a flag, red, white and blue. His sled has flags on each side, and his Reindeer wear little hats made of flags. Flags are sprouting up everywhere. They are back in the windows of Central High. People are putting up flag poles, and the couple in the house down the street make quite a ritual of taking down "Old Glory" just before night fall each day.

We are having a second patriotic Christmas, but no longer is it clear who or what we are fighting, or protecting, or mourning. Last year I guess the flags were about the victims and heroes of 9/11, and maybe about supporting American soldiers in Afghanistan. This year I'm not sure who the flags are for. I guess they just mark our endless war against the terrorists.

But it does not matter who the flags are for. The effect of all of these waving flags in all of these windows, on all these car and pick-up windows, in all those stores and store fronts, is to say that Americans are patriotic, that God is on Our Side. As we enter Year Two of Bush's War, to raise a question about the flags, any question, is to risk being called unpatriotic. But then how do we celebrate patriotism in this new war, when the war is taking away the very freedoms and ideals the flag stands for?

* * * * * * * * * * *

Orem, Utah, 1 December 2002

The *New York Times* reports on a debate about the war with Iraq. In the first-period social studies class at Lakeridge Junior High school in Orem, Utah, students in Donell Willey's world studies class debate the war, taking sides, for and against Bush: "The President is doing this for political gain;" "The Administration has the right to act quickly;" "The Constitution says we the people, not we the government. You can't just let the President decide things on his own"; "Killing Saddam Hussein won't bring a solution"; "These are career terrorists. They only way to stop them is to put them away for good" (Clemetson, 2002, p. 20).

* * * * * * * * * * *

And this so-called "just war" against evil continues. Another headline and story, this from Summer 2002.

Collateral Damage: Oruzgan, Afghanistan

New York Times, Saturday, 6 July, front page. A photograph of a gravesite, rocks piled high on the brown earth. A young man named Abdul Malik stands looking at the fresh graves of his family. Abdul lost 25 members of his family, including his mother and father to an American air attack, on 1 July. He and his family were celebrating a wedding. It started innocently enough, children in the village setting of firecrackers and men firing rifles into the air in accordance with local traditions. Suddenly American bombers appeared from nowhere. Bombs were dropped on four villages. Forty-eight civilians were killed, 117 injured. U. S. Military headquarters called the loss collateral damage, contending it was part of the cost of fighting terrorism and ridding Afghanistan of the Taliban and Al Quaeda. American military officials stated that an American AC-130 had been fired upon by antiaircraft emplacements (Bumiller, 2002, p. Al).

* * * * * * * * * * *

6 July 2002. Kennebunkport

Bush offfers apology: President Bush called President Hamid Karzal of Afghanistan today to express his sympathies, but not to apologize for the American bombing raid. Later in the day the President celebrated his 56th birthday at a party with family members at their Walker's Point compound. He went boating and fishing with his father.

10 July 2002

America military officials admit the attack on the villages was not an accident, contending they had ground-level evidence that high-ranking members of Al

Quaeda were in the region. So much for those smart bombs and that new satellite communications system.

* * * * * * * * * *

The war goes on

What are people reading these days? My local library weekly posts the list of Best Sellers, as reported in the *New York Times* Book Review. This week there are three books on the list about life in America after 9/11/01. The books include Rudolph Giuliani's *Leadership*, a discussion of what it takes to be a leader after 9/11; *Let's Roll*, by Lisa Beamer, a memoir by the wife of Todd Beamer, one of the passengers on United Flight 93, the hijacked jet that crashed in Pennsylvania on September 11; *Let Freedom Ring* by Sean Hannity, a conservative commentary on domestic and foreign issues after 9/11; and last week Bob Woodward published *Bush's War*, a year-long look at how Bush and his administration managed America's war against terrorism.

* * * * * * * * * *

So life after 9/11 has become more complex, as we glide from one war into another. And 9/11 itself has become more complicated, folded into the flag, commodified, packaged, sold, worn on one's lapel, waved in the front yard. 9/11 everywhere you look. Bush's legacy, unlimited patriotism, unending war, everyday something new to lose your mind over, the evils of this insane world seem unfathomable. Laurel Richardson (2002, p. 25) asks, "How can we make sense of this war for children, if we cannot explain it to ourselves?"

* * * * * * * * * *

Maybe Annie Dillard (1974, p. 270) is right, maybe the universe was not made in jest, but I need more. I need hope, I need to believe that the world is a just place to live, that there are just people in this world. I need places to go where I can experience solace, and peace, a presence of mind that is not haunted by pictures of young men standing by gravel and stone graves, wondering why their mother and father are dead. I need a just government. I need and dream of a government that shows in its performances how we can create a peaceful, nonviolent world, a world where there are no just wars, a world where words like freedom, happiness, human rights, care, justice and equality have real meaning, a world without end, a radical, utopian world, a world filled with hope, and dreams of peace not yet dreamed. A world that has no place for Bush and his wars, and his flags.

* * * * * * * * * * *

References

Bumiller, Elisabeth. (2002, July 6). Bush Offers Karzai Sympathy on Dead. *New York Times*, pp. A-1, A6: 20.

Clemetson, Lynette. (2002, December 1). Debate on War With Iraq Is Entering the Classroom. *New York Times*, p. A-20.

Dillard, Annie. (1974). *Pilgrim at Tinker Creek.* New York: Harper & Row.

Richardson, Laurel. (2002). "Small World." *Cultural Studies—Critical Methodologies*, 2, (1): 23–25.

5

Week 73: Good People and Dirty Work

(3-4-03)

Week Seventy-Three of the War on Terrorism

America's on-ending war against terrorism is in week seventy-three. Newspaper headlines report such items as the following:

* President Bush now talks as if the war in Iraq is over, while making plans for democratizing the Middle East;
* Even so, Turkey, a democratic nation, refuses to let American troops land;
* Baghdad destroys missiles;
* A major leader of Al Qaeda is captured in Pakistan;
* The United Emirates ask Saddam Hussein to leave power to avert a war;
* Estimates of the size of world-wide anti-war protests on 15 February range from 8–12 million, making this the single largest mobilization against war in history. Over 100 American city councils, including Los Angeles and Chicago, have passed anti-war resolutions;
* President Bush refuses to listen to the protesters, contending that to do so would be like deciding policy based upon a focus group;

* Last week the new Office for Homeland Security was formally launched;
* The Justice Department proposes to extend powers granted under the 2001 U. S. A. Patriot Act, including:
    invalidating state legal consent decrees that curb police spying;
    allowing the collection of DNA materials from suspected terrorists by such means as are necessary. Failing to cooperate would be a crime;
    allowing citizenship to be stripped from people who support groups that the U. S. considers terrorist organizations (Clymer, 2003).

* * *

Last week, Americans were urged to prepare disaster supply kits including duct tape to seal windows against airborne toxins.

* * *

President Bush seems to be at peace with himself, as America continues its permanent war against the rest of the world.

* * *

Frank Rich (2003) speaks of the fixed ideas and certain truths that have been implemented by the Bush Administration since 9/11/01:

* In this time of crisis Americans now need to watch what they say, and watch what they do;
* President Bush is acting with moral clarity, his critics are anti-American;
* From a marketing point of view you do not introduce a new product like a war in Iraq in August;
* In order to remain free, we must give up basic freedoms.

* * *

The new Homeland Security Act requires all universities to record the activities of their male non-resident international students on SEVIS, otherwise known as the Student Exchange Visitor Information System. SEVIS went online 30 January 2003. This system links university databases with the INS, the FBI and the CIA (Kien, 2003)

* * *

In 1948 sociologist Everett C. Hughes visited postwar Germany, interviewing Germans about the Nazis and their treatment of several million Jews in the concentration camps. His essay (1963) 'Good People and Dirty Work', presents facts and stories about perhaps the most dramatic piece of dirty work the world has ever known. Hughes asked how all these good people in Germany could have stood by and allowed the dirty work of the Nazis to have taken place. How could all these good people live in the midst of such cruelty? Why was there not a general uprising against "it and the people who did it?" (p. 25). And, once freed from the "regime that did it, how could they be apparently so little concerned about it, so toughly silent about it?" (p. 25). Further, how could you find, in today's civilized societies, people who would engage in such vile, violent, dirty work? How could such persons be released from the inhibitions of civilized life "so as to be able to imagine, let alone perform, the ferocious, obscene and perverse actions which they did imagine and perform?" How could a group of people be kept at a "height of fury" (p. 25), that would lead them to persist and endure, even as they were "literally spattered with the human filth and waste produced by their own actions" (p. 25). How did these good people talk themselves into doing this dirty work?

As systems like SEVIS are implemented, and as the government seeks more power under the U. S. Patriot and Homeland Security Acts, Hughes's observations on good people and dirty work seem as relevant today as they were in 1963.

* * *

Observations of potential dirty work:

Scene One: Regional Airport: Thirty men and women wearing the new homeland security administration uniforms gaze down from a balcony on three citizens waiting in line for their boarding passes. The citizens look up at the men and women watching them.

Scene Two: Regional Airport: A female traveler is taken aside and asked to raise her arms and spread her legs as an electronic wand is passed over her body. She smiles at the security attendant, who apologizes for embarrassing her.

Scene Three: Regional Airport: This same female traveler is now asked to stand aside as her suitcase is opened, and the wand is inserted into the luggage. The security attendant removes items from the suitcase, as he examines it. He apologizes to her, and his supervisor says, "This will not take long."

Scene Four: Regional Airport: A middle-aged male traveler walks through the electronic gates and sets off an alarm. He is told to step back, to remove his belt, to take off his shoes, and to open his shirt. He then walks back through the electronic gates in his stocking feet, while holding up his pants, The two security attendants smile at him, perhaps acknowledging the awkwardness of the situation.

* * *

In telling his story of good people and dirty work Hughes is quick to point out that he is not attempting to make the Germans look worse than other peoples. He intends, rather, to "recall to our attention dangers which lurk in our midst always" (p. 23). In talking with the German people, Hughes learned that many were unwilling and afraid to think of or even talk about the atrocities. Many did not know of the gory details, which were kept secret. Indeed, the S. S. was a secret society, and it kept its dirty work out of view. Many good people felt the pain of the Jews and attempted to make their ghastly situations as humane as possible. Deep down some experienced terror and fear, and guilt, for they felt that what was done was incorrect.

* * *

Today it seems that we are all good people doing dirty work, acknowledging through our own willing complicity with a system that is stripping us of our human, civil rights. Nobody is really happy about this, except maybe the newly employed security attendants, as well as President Bush, Tommy Ridge and John Ashcroft.

In submitting to these rituals of public degradation, we announce a commitment to homeland security. None of us really believe, though, that these strip-searches will lead to the discovery of a terrorist bomber. At least this has not happened yet. So the strip-search functions to affirm President Bush's war on terrorism. By participating in these searches we become members of his army of volunteer citizens who are fighting this evil which lurks in our midst. And sadly, in this participation, like Germany's good people, we partake in the selfsame dirty work that we abhor in others.

References

Clymer, Adam. (2003, February 8). "Domestic Security: Justice Department Draft on Wider Powers Draws Quick Criticism." *New York Times*, p. A-9.

Hughes, Everett C. 1963. "Good People and Dirty Work." Pp. 23–36. In Howard S. Becker (Ed.), *The Other Side: Perspectives on Deviance*, pp.23–36. New York: Free Press.

Kien, Grant. (2003). "Sevis: Liebniz Meets Bush." *The public i.* 3(2): 7.

Rich, Frank. (2003, March 13). On 'Fixed Ideas' Since September 11. *New York Review of Books,* Vol. L, 20.

6

Week 75: Democracy is a Gift

(4-16-03)

Week 75, Day 525 of the War on Terrorism

America's on-ending war against terrorism is in its 75th week, day 525. America continues its permanent war against the world. My depression deepens. I'm addicted to CNN and its permanent report on the war against terror. Somehow I think the televised images of the Iraqi war will discredit Bush and his administration, and its doctrine of preemptive strikes against nations in the Axis of Evil. But such is not the case.

I must turn elsewhere, for this depression is affecting my work and my life.

On the 525th day of this war, headlines and stories in the morning *New York Times* read:

* Bush says Regime in Iraq is No More; Victory is 'Certain';
* Free to Protest, Iraqis Complain About U.S. : 'Down, Down U.S.A.—- don't stay, go away!';
* Defense Secretary Rumsfeld said U.S. was moving to cut off an important oil pipeline running from Iraq to Syria;
* Coalition forces guard oil fields while the national museums are ransacked, and precious heirlooms from a 7000 year-old civilization are looted and destroyed ;

* Secretary Rumsfeld says you can not blame the war plan for the looting; "such things are hard to stop in the war zone;"
* Mr. Bush said he plans to make the new Iraq a model of democracy in the Middle East.

* * *

Day 525, 7:15 am. It is not enough to be against the war. The way out of this depression is to think utopian, radical thoughts of peace, to get over mourning the loss of democracy in America. I need to turn away from CNN, and the *New York Times*.

Norman Mailer (2003) says that we cannot bring democracy to Iraq by invasion. Democracy, he observes, "is never in us to to create in another country by the force of our will" (p. 52). Democracy is not a commodity that can be bought and sold, or carried on the backs of military troops.

Walt Whitman (1993) said that America is the world's best and most radical experiment in democracy. He sought a political poetic that would embody the spiritual and moral themes of an egalitarian democratic order. He sought a wild, free, open poetic, a poetry that joyfully sings songs of passion, exuberant songs that celebrate the beauty of democracy's wild soul, songs that mourn democracy's death, poems that dwell on those painful days when lilacs no longer bloom in the dooryard.

Real democracy, Whitman and Mailer remind us, comes from the soul. Real democracy is bonedeep. It is sutured into the moral fibers of the person. It saturates the landscapes and public spheres of daily life. Real democracy is more than a political ideology, or a set of procedures for electing officials who represent the will of the people. A truly free democracy is not forged in the crucibles of violence or battle. Democracy is peaceful and non-violent. Democracy cannot be forcefully inserted into the soul of another person or nation.

Democracy must be indigenous to a nation and its moral landscapes. It must be grounded in many subtle individual and group experiences that extend over generations, decades, centuries, lifetimes (Mailer, 2003, p. 52). Obviously the only defenses "of democracy . . . are the traditions of democracy" (Mailer, 2003, p. 52). It is an oxymoron to assert that the violent overthrow of a government can be justified in the name of protecting democracy. This is not defending democracy, this is using force to impose one nation's will on the will of another nation. Democracy must come from within the soul of a nation.

Democracy is a fragile and delicate thing, "it is always endangered, it is a state of grace" (Mailer, 2003, p. 52).

Mailer thinks that the natural government for most people, "given the uglier depths of human nature, is fascism" (p. 52). Too many people in America today, it seems, seek and value the symbols, certainty, power, rhetoric, ideology and violence that fascism offers. Fascism is democracy's natural enemy. In America today, fascism has won. Democracy's delicate petals have been crushed. America and democracy have fallen from grace.

Whitman mourned the death of Lincoln, and what that death meant for a divided nation, and he wrote "When Lilacs Last In the Dooryard Bloom'd." I mourn democracy's death in America, and I want to write a ode to freedom that soars overhead, like a wild Whitman poem. I fear for those in Iraq who will be victims of American military fascism, a fascism that stands by while cultural icons and sacred religious texts are destroyed, and the American flag waves high over head.

* * *

Thus does Whitman lead me out of my depression; I withdraw from my song for myself. I seek a song for others that builds on democracy's promise, "Lilac and star and bird twined with the chant of my soul" (Whitman, 1993, p. 294). Thousands of doves of peace fly from America to Iraq, crushing and refusing President Bush's flag-waving project to make the new Iraq a model for democracy in the Middle East. Lilacs will again bloom in the dooryard.

References

Mailer, Norman. (2003, . March 27) "Only in America." *New York Review of Books*, 50, (5), 49–53.

Whitman, Walt. (1993). *Leaves of Grass and Selected Prose*. London: J. M. Dent, Orion Publishing Group.

7

Week 93: The War on Culture, the War on Truth, Part I

(6-18-03)

"I will never apologize for the United States—I don't care what the facts are"
(George Bush, Sr. quoted in Roy, 2003, p. 77).[1]

"Intelligence gathered by this and other governments leaves no doubt that the Iraq regime continues to possess and conceal some of the most lethal weapons ever devised"
(George W. Bush, 17 March 2003).

Today, violence, it seems, is everywhere, democracy is under attack, America is engaged in a war without end, a permanent war on the world. This is the space we inhabit. It is appropriate that cultural studies scholars police the current international situation crisis (Denzin and Lincoln, 2003, p. xv). Culture and the critical methodologies used for producing truth are two of the major casualities in America's war with Iraq. Manipulating its versions of geo-political reality, the Bush administration has constructed a violent politics of truth concerning America and the so-called threats by terrorists to democracy and freedom.

This policing of the crisis, accordingly, must move in four directions at the same time, starting with and always returning to the personal and the biographical, the cultural and the social, the human tragedies in a post 9/11 world.

Critical discourse, secondly, must continue to be directed at the media, the Presidency, and the ideological discourses surrounding America's permanent war on terrorists. Thirdly, conversations, mutterings, and dialogues about peace, justice, war, and the shrinking of civil liberties and social justice in America and abroad must get louder and continue until a progressive president is in office (Schell, 2003, p. 6). Fourth, there has never been a greater need for critical, interpretive methodologies that can help us make sense of life in an age of the hyperreal, the simulacra, TV wars, staged media events, Top Gun escapades by a President who avoided the Vietnam draft.

The Bush regime uses its version of truth and reality as an excuse for armed aggression. In turn, the slogan "War Is Peace" (Roy, 2001c, p. 125) justifies collateral damage, the loss of lives and culture caused by the weapons of war (and peace). Such losses are regrettably necessary, if the world is to be made safer and more peaceful. It is irrelevant if the evidence supporting armed aggression does not stand up in a court of law (Roy, 2001c, p. 126), America is on a mission, centuries of jurisprudence will not stand in our way (Roy, 2001c, p. 126) And so concepts of justice, truth and law are "carelessly trashed" (Roy, 2001c, p. 126). In the meantime attacks on G. I. s and key industrial sites are on the rise in Iraq.

The positive benefits of regime change are slipping out of sight, squandered on a daily basis. Iraqi citizens struggle to return to a normal pre-war life, but everywhere they turn they confront violence, gun fire, soaring prices, food shortages, scarce money, long lines for gasoline. Electricity, telephones, TV, public transportation, sanitary, medical and water services are sporadic. Schools remain closed, civil servants are out of work. Suspicious of the Americans and fearful of their presence, post-liberation Iraqis are "too scarred by the past, too wary of the future to believe that their long nightmare may have ended" (Rodenbeck, 2003, p. 23).

Iraq looks like a ravaged landscape; looters, ransacked buildings, broken glass, broken windows, blown-out walls, concrete craters in the center of streets, rotting heaps of garbage, rats, fecal stench; borrowed generators produce flickering light, shadows of despair in a darkening gloom, scene after scene of devastation. Outside the deserted National Library in Baghdad a "tethered donkey lunches on flowers in the garden. A statue of Saddam is still standing out front" (Rodenbeck, 2003, p. 22). Partially hidden by a row of American tanks, the scene seems "too staged to be true" (Rodenbeck, 2003, p. 22).

The Bush administration must be held doubly accountable for these events, these scenes of destruction. It owes America and the world an accounting for how it mislead the nation into the Iraqi war. It owes the Iraqis an apology for the loss of thousands of Iraqi lives, all apparently justified in the name of American national security (Krugman, 2003, p. A27).

Destroying Culture

The failure of the Bush administration to stop the desecration of Iraq's museums is inexplicable. Words can barely describe the feelings of pain and anger that are felt. It as if we are bearing witness to the death of a great civilization. Photographs depict the willful destruction of Iraqi art and material culture. How did the Bush administration allow this to happen? They were given ample warning that precautions needed to be taken if the sacred texts and material objects from this ancient culture were not to be destroyed in the war. But nothing was done. This bespeaks a callousness and an arrogance that are deplorable and unacceptable. Is this what American democracy stands for?

In the Baghdad museum alone it is estimated that between 2000 and 3000 pieces of art are missing, or destroyed. The entire "two million volumes of the National Library and Archives are ash" (Rich, 2003, p. 34). The American military guarded the oil wells of Iraq, but not the Iraqi museums.

With the death of culture in Iraq comes violence, and a new American enemy, one of our own making. The Iraqis do not want us in their country. In his recent Middle East trip President Bush did not land in Baghdad because his aids decided it was too risky; "a warm welcome from Iraqis was far from assured" (Sanger, 2003, p. A13). Instead the President viewed the city from six miles up out of the windows of Air Force One.

The Iraqis are expressing their rejection of U.S. occupation through violence and looting. As this happens, the coalition army is growing, not shrinking. It is estimated that the U. S. will spend over $40 billion to finance the Iraqi war and the ongoing occupation, while allocating $16 billion to U. S. welfare and education programs.

The War On Truth

Ignoring international opinion and discounting thousands of war protesters, Bush launched his war against Iraq, declaring "I do not decide policy based on focus groups" (Purdum, 2003, p. 5). The Iraqi regime poses an imminent threat to America. We must go to war. And so Bush presented the world with photographs, statistics, and quotes from intelligence sources confirming Iraq's links to Al Qaeda, suggesting that Saddam might have been behind the tragedies of 9/11, and that he was harboring terrorists and sitting on lethal weapons of mass destruction.

As of 17 June 2003, no chemical laboratories or weapons of mass destruction have been found. Nor is there any evidence supporting the alleged connection between Saddam and Al Qaeda. Critics clamor that the threats were made up. But Bush counters these criticisms, pledging to the troops in Iraq that, "We're on the look, we'll reveal the truth " (Neikirk, 2003, p. 1). But the truth cannot be revealed. It can only be represented. The Bush Administration has been searching for nearly a year to find this evidence which apparently does not exist.

However, the evidence no longer needs to be produced. Under the current regime of truth, the terms of the argument have changed. Just a week ago (9 June 2003) President Bush challenged his critics, "The credibility of the United States is based on our strong desire to make the world more peaceful, and the world is more peaceful after our decision" (Bush quoted in Stevenson and Risen, 2003, p. A10).

But we did not go to war to make the world more peaceful. We went to war to remove Saddam because he had weapons of mass destruction. Surely Iraq is not a more peaceful place to live in after Bush's decision. Under the terms of his logic, the U.S. expresses its credibility and desire for peace by going to war. War Is Peace. Black is white. Red is green, girls are boys (Roy, 2001c, p. 127). America is a peaceful nation. We are a peaceful people. We go to war to wage peace.

Meanwhile, British Prime Minister Tony Blair, America's strongest wartime ally, comes under increasing pressure to prove that he and Bush did not lie to the world community. Skeptics are suggesting that "top officials in the U. S. and Britain misrepresented intelligence reports on Iraq's capabilities to make Hussein's regime appear to be more of a threat than it was" (Neikirk, 2003, p. 1). Some are saying they cooked the intelligence.

As it imposes its will on the world, the Bush administration manipulates reality. It stages situations, lies, fabricates, uses forged documents, exaggerates threats, manipulates symbols, invokes patriotism, asserts that critics are unpatriotic—criticism aids the enemy. Truth, culture, and lives are the victims in this regime. Secretary of Defense Rumsfeld argues that America will have won its new war, if "we can convince the world that Americans must be allowed to continue their way of life" (Roy, 2001b, pp. 119–120). This victory apparently involves getting the world community to believe that War Is Peace.

Truth, Protest, and Policing the Crisis

Cultural studies scholars have a moral obligation to confront the current situation, to speak to the death of lives, culture, and truth, to undo the official pedagogies that circulate in the media (see Denzin and Lincoln, 2003). What is happening in the world today lies outside "the realm of human understanding" (Roy 2001a, p. 32). It is up to the poets, the writers, the artists, and scholars in cultural studies to make sense of what is happening. We need testimonies, autoethnographies, performance texts, new stories, plays, and dramas about real people with real lives, the horror of it all. "Stories about what its like to lose your home, your land, your job, your dignity, your past and your future to an invisible force. To someone or something you can't see" (Roy, 2001a, p. 32). We need stories about what it is like to hate and feel despair, anger, and alienation about a world that has gone insane. We need pedagogical discourses that make these feelings visible, palpable, stories and performances that connect these emotions to wild utopian dreams of freedom and peace.

Stealing a line from Roy (2001a, p. 32), we are inside a shabby deal, a deal gone bad on a global scale, a failed revolution involving power politics. We are witnessing the collapse of the corporate, neo-liberal globalization project, the death of old-fashioned imperialism, the death of the new Empire.

And so we seek a new politics of resistance, and truth, a politics of opposition, a world-wide joining of hands, the globalization of dissent (Roy, 2001a, p. 33). A new day, a refusal by humankind to allow men to any longer make and wage war in the name of vainglory, profit, and corrupt political ideologies (Sontag, 2003, p. 3).

In the age of dramaturgy and TV wars, critical pedagogies and interpretive methodologies of truth must be assessed in terms of their ability to produce love, justice, empowerment, and freedom. Deceit and deception have no place in these moral spaces. Critical methodologies must exhibit interpretive sufficiency, be free of racial, class, or gender stereotyping, rely on multiple voices, enhance moral discernment, promote social transformation, and critical consciousness (Christians, 2000, p. 145; Denzin, 2003, p. 112). A politics of liberation can be built on discourses that embody these guidelines. Such politics provide a platform for mobilizing dissent, for undoing the neoliberal empire and its racist, repressive agenda.

We must continue to address the moral acts of those who would act on our behalf. We must resist the forces of fascism, and rebel against knee-jerk patriotism. We must expose the injustices of capitalism while protesting wars waged in its name. We must seek non-violent regimes of truth that honor culture, universal human rights, and the sacred. We must seek critical methodologies that protest, resist and help us represent and imagine radically free utopian spaces.

* * *

I need hope, pedagogies of love, not war (Darder, 2002). Walt Whitman and Paulo Freire help me.

> I sit and look out upon the sorrows of the world, and upon all
> oppression and shame,
> I hear secret convulsive sobs . . .
> I observe the slights and degradations cast by arrogant persons . . .
> All these—all the meanness and agony without end I sitting look
> out upon,
> See, hear, and am silent (Whitman,1860/1994, p. 240).

* * *

But silent no longer. To remain silent is to be in collusion with this immoral political regime, to remain silent is to allow evil to happen.

Note

1. Bush made these remarks in "refusing to apologize for the shooting down of an Iranian passenger plane, killing 290 passengers" (Roy, 2003, p. 77).

References

Christians, Clifford. (2000). Ethics and Politics in Qualitative Research. In Norman K. Denzin and Yvonna S. Lincoln (Eds.), *Handbook of Qualitative Research*, 2/e. (pp. 133–155.) Thousand Oaks, CA: Sage.

Denzin, Norman K. (2003). *Performance Ethnography: Critical Pedagogy and the Politics of Culture*. Thousand Oaks: Sage.

Darder, Antonia, (2002). *Reinventing Paulo Freire: A Pedagogy of Love*. Boulder, Colorado: Westview Press.

Denzin, Norman K. and Yvonna S. Lincoln. (2003). "Introduction: 9/11 in American Culture." In Norman K. Denzin and Yvonna S. Lincoln (Eds.), *9/11in American Culture.* (pp. xiii–xvii) Walnut Creek: Altamira Press.

Krugman, Paul. (2003, June 10). Who's Accountable?. *New York Times*, p. A27.

Neikirk, William. (2003, June 6). Bush Pledges to Reveal the Truth. *Chicago Tribune*, p. 1.

Purdum, Todd S. (2003, February 23). Focus Groups?: To Bush Crowds Were a Blur. *New York Times*, p. WK: 5.

Rich, Frank. (2003, June 1). George W. Bush and the Poet. *New York Times*, Arts and Leisure: pp. 1, 34.

Rodenbeck, Max. (2003, July 3). Bohemia in Baghdad. *New York Review of Books*, 50, (11): 20–23.

Roy, Arundhati. (2001a). The Ladies Have Feelings, So . . . Shall We Leave It to the Experts? In Arundhati Roy, *Power Politics*, (pp. 1–34). Cambridge, Mass: South End Press.

Roy, Arundhati. (2001b). The Algebra of Infinite Justice. In Arundhati Roy, *Power Politics*, (Pp. 105–124). Cambridge, Mass: South End Press.

Roy, Arundhati. (2001c). War Is Peace. In Arundhati Roy, *Power Politics*, (*pp.* 125–145). Cambridge, Mass: South End Press.

Roy, Arundhati. (2003). The Loneliness of Noam Chomsky. In *War Talk*, (pp. 77–101). Cambridge, Mass: South End Press.

Sanger, David S. (2003, June 6). Bush Tells Troops the Truth Will Emerge About Weapons Hidden by Hussein. *New York Times*, p. A13.

Schell, Jonathan. (2003, June 23). "Thinking Movement, Working Demonstration." *The Nation*. 276, (24): 6.

Sontag, Susan. (2003, June 1). *Regarding the Pain of Others*. New York: Farrar, Straus, and Giroux.

Stevenson, Richard W. and James Resin. (2003, June 10). Bush Again Vows U. S. Will Find Illicit Weapons. *New York Times*, A10.

Tyler, Patrick E. (2003, June 1). There's a New Enemy in Iraq: The Nasty Surprise. *New York Times*, p. WK: 5.

Whitman, Walt. 1994/1860. I Sit and Look Out. In *Leaves of Grass*, (p. 210). London: J. M. Dent: Everyman

8

Week 93: Iraq and the World Go Sour, Part II

(11-20-03)

In making sense of the current historical moment, when Iraq and the world seem to have gone sour (*New York Times*, 2003), and the Bush administration appears to be without a plan, I follow Benjamin's advice about writing history under a fascist regime. Such histories consist of a series of quotations, documents and texts placed side-by-side, producing a de-centered narrative, a multi-voiced text with voices and speakers speaking back and forth, often past one another.

Benjamin's histories rip the present out of its present context, refusing to privilege the past for fascism's history only unfolds as a series of interconnected presents, one crisis, one catastrophe, one state of alert, one national emergency seamlessly knitted into the next. Quoting the present back to itself exposes these contradictions and ruptures in the fascist project (Benjamin, 1983, p. 24; 1968, pp. 255–266). The story of Bush's administration has been the story of one crisis after another, starting with 9/11/01, moving then from one war to the next (Corn, 2003).

I offer a selective representation of Bush statements on the war in Iraq, reading Bush back against himself, exposing just a few of the cracks in his war project. I insert these representations in a ruptured, unruly multi-voiced text. This is a play of sorts, a short drama with several voices, including Bush's, whom

I place in an imaginary conversation with Walter Benjamin, who had much to say about the forces of fascism in his day.

Prelude to A One-Act Play: Theses on the Philosophy of History According to George W. Bush

Preamble:

VOICE # 1: AUTHOR AS NARRATOR:

Can there be any truth to the lies George W. Bush tells?

VOICE # 2: WALTER BENJAMIN (PARAPHRASED):

You can never recover the truth of the past, only images, memories (Benjamin, 1968, p. 257; Ulmer, 1989, p. 111).

VOICE # 3: TOM CRUISE:

"Oh, you mean like when George played dress up and imitated me on that battleship?

VOICE # 4: WALTER BENJAMIN (PARAPHRASED):

Yup! You can never tell his history exactly the way it was.

That's correct. There will always be his version of history, and your version (Moore, 2003; Corn, 2003; Ivins, 2003).

VOICE # 5: WALTER BENJAMIN, PART 2:

You must turn Bush's white patriarchal, crony capitalist history back against him. Confront him with his lies, show that truthiness is not the same thing as telling the truth. Do your version of the Comedy Hour—put the quotes up on the screen, Make a spectacle of their lies. Show that their lies are killing people

VOICE # 6: GEORGE W. BUSH:

I told no lies. I tell the truth. It doesn't matter that there were no WMDs. I never said there were. I have always told the truth, even when I had to lie, Because if I had told the truth, people would not have believed me.

References

Benjamin, Walter. (1968). *Illuminations.* Trans. Harry Zohn. New York: Harcourt, Brace & World, Inc.

Benjamin, Walter. (1983). N Theoretics of Knowledge: Theory of Progress. *The Philosophical Forum* 15.

Corn, David. (2003). *The Lies of George W. Bush: Mastering the Politics of Deception*. New York: Crown Publishers.

Ivins, Molly with Lou Dubose. (2003). *Bushwacked: Life in Geroge W. Bush's America*. New York: Random House.

Moore, Michael. (2003). *Dude, Where's My Country*. New York: Warner Books.

Editorial: Iraq Goes Sour. (2003, November 16). *New York Times*. Editorials/Letters, p. 12.

Pope, Carl.(2003, November, December). Big Pigs at the Trough: The Worst Agriculture Policy Money Can Buy. *Sierra*, 88, (8): 8–9.

Powers, Thomas. (2003, December 4). The Vanishing Case for War. *The New York Review of Books*,50, (19): 12–17

Ulmer, Gregory. (1989). *Teletheory: Grammatology in the Age of Video*. New York: Routledge.

9

Week 110: Shame and Despair in December

(12-16-03)

Dateline: Champaign, Illinois: Week 110, Day 777 of the War on Terrorism

Bush's war continues. Like a fog it is everywhere. It cannot be escaped, nor can it be contained. Indeed, on a daily basis, there are new assaults on our senses, new attacks on human rights, education, justice, the environment, social security, medicare, welfare, energy, women's rights, affirmative action, gay marriages. Sample the headlines of *The New York Times*. Hiding behind 9/11, the conservatives intend to impose their will, and morality, on every corner of American society.

Policing this crisis has become nearly impossible, although "latest@daily.misleader. org" and "moveon. org." help with their daily listing of Bush's latest lie (see also Corn, 2003; Moore, 2003; Ivins, 2003; Franken, 2003). I'm embarrassed. I'm ashamed. I feel despair. What does it mean to be an American in times such as this? Consider these paraphrased headlines:

- As the guerrilla war against Iraqi insurgents intensifies, American soldiers have begun wrapping entire villages in barbed wire. *A sign reads*: "This fence is here for your protection. Do not approach or try to cross, or you will be shot."

* "With a heavy dose of fear and violence, and a lot of money for projects, I think we can convince these people that we are here to help them" (American battalion commander).
* Afghan villagers torn by grief after U. S. air strike kills 9 children. . . The intended target escaped . . . The American military command expressed regret for the killings.
* High payments to Haliburton for fuel in Irag. The US government is paying the Haliburton Company an average of $2.64 a gallon to import gasoline and other fuel to Iraq from Kuwait, more than twice what others are paying . . . It appears that Haliburton has been charging the US government and Iraq's oil-for-food program an average of about $1.60 a gallon for fuel available for 71 cents wholesale.
* Pentagon bars three nations from Iraq bids—war opponents punished. Lucrative contracts will be denied to Germany, France, and Russia.

* * *

Where do we go next? Barbed wire around villages? Heavy doses of fear and violence? Air strikes on Afghan villages? Is there no end to the fraud, the scandals, the arrogance, the insensitivity to the pain we are causing others?

* * *

I turn to Mark Twain for help. He captures my feelings best in his 1898 essay, "A Word of Encouragement for our Blushing Exiles" (Twain, 1963b). Written in opposition to the Spanish-American War, and America's invasion of Cuba (and later the Philippines), Twain observes: "And so you are ashamed . . . Apparently you are ashamed to look Europe in the face; ashamed of the American name; temporarily ashamed of your nationality" (1963b, pp. ,682–83). He judges that the exiles are ashamed because:

1. "We are meddling where we have no business and no right; meddling with the private family matters of a sister nation; intruding upon her sacred rights.
2. We are doing this under a sham humanitarian pretext.
3. Doing it to filch Cuba, the formal and distinct disclaimer in the ultimatum being very, very thin humbug, and easily detectable as such by you and virtuous Europe.

4. And finally you are ashamed of all this because it is new, and base, and brutal, and dishonest; and because Europe . . . is horrified by it and can never respect us nor associate with us any more" (Twain, 1963b, p. 683).

* * *

Yes, I am ashamed, and for all of the reasons listed by Twain. America is involved in a fraudulent war. There were no weapons of mass destruction. There is no connection between al Qaeda, Bin Laden and Saddam Hussein.

Locked in a time capsule, this could be 1893. I scarcely need to change a word in Twain's indictment of US foreign policy. Paraphrasing only slightly, today we too bear witness to events that are brutal, base, dreadful, dishonest, and ruthless. We have launched a Reign of Terror in the Middle East. Our armies are slaughtering innocent human beings. Our politicians tell lies. We are not winning the war; what war? We are losing the respect of the entire world community.

We are acting like land thieves in Iraq, standing by as ancient cultural artifacts are destroyed. We are acting in shabby ways, outraging people of honor, adding yet another chapter to a shameful history of foreign robberies and humanitarian shams (Twain, 1963b, p. 683).

Bush is today's version of Twain's Professional Official Fibber. Bush, America's Official Fibber, speaking to television reporters, tells lies with a straight face. "No, we did not arrange the media event on board the U. S. Lincoln announcing the end of the war," Bush states, without missing a beat. "This is something our brave fighting men did." The Official Fibber divides reality into two categories: Absolute Good and Absolute Evil. Communists have been replaced by terrorists. Terrorists are evil thugs because they hate America because we stand for freedom (Stam, 2003, p. 27). The Official Fibber says black is white, that we are winning a war we are losing. The Official Fibber says the economy is turning around when another 50,000 Americans lost their jobs last month. The Professional Official Fibber will do anything to stay in power.

Indicting the press, Twain asks, "Is there a way out of this calamity?" We cannot rely on the media to get us out this mess because they are part of the problem. Clearly Bush's lies can no longer be allowed. Under his regime the meaning of the word democracy has been forever tarnished.

Being ashamed and being angry are no longer enough. If we are going to make it through December, stealing a line from Merle Haggard, we must resist this fraudulent, fascist, violent regime. We must make performative spectacles of this regime's lies and deceptions, exposing the cracks and contradictions that hold it together. Our fragile democracy requires no less. We must resist.

* * *

Here is an example. The following short play, a ruptured, unruly, multi-voiced text, is one form this resistance may take, one way of making sense of the current historical moment, when Iraq and the world seem to have gone sour (*New York Times*, 2003) and the Bush Administration appears to be without a plan. This short drama has several voices, including Tom Cruise, Molly Ivins, Carl Pope, bell hooks, Walt Whitman, Paulo Freire, David Corn, and George Bush. Bush is placed in an imaginary conversation with Walter Benjamin, and Mark Twain, both of whom had much to say about the forces of fascism in their day.[1]

A One-Act Play: Theses on the Philosophy of History According to George W. Bush

VOICE # 1: AUTHOR AS NARRATOR:

My fellow Americans, let us begin this short history of the present with the understanding that there is a truth to the lies of George W. Bush. Men, women and children are dying in Bush's dirty little war in Iraq, and it is costing us over 4 billion dollars a week.

VOICE # 2: WALTER BENJAMIN (PARAPHRASED):

To articulate the past historically does not mean to recognize it the way it really was. It means to seize hold of a memory as it flashes up in a moment of danger, of anger, of despair, (Benjamin, 1968, p. 257; Ulmer, 1989, p. 111).

VOICE # 3: TOM CRUISE:

Oh, you mean like when George imitated me, got dressed up like a fighter pilot and acted like he was Mr. 'Top Gun' and said the war was over in Iraq—you mean a memory and an image like that?

VOICE # 4: WALTER BENJAMIN (PARAPHRASED):

Yes, exactly!

VOICE # 5: AUTHOR AS NARRATOR:

O. K. I've lived through three years of Bush as President. Does this mean that I can never tell his history like it really was?

VOICE # 6: WALTER BENJAMIN:

That's correct. There will always be his version of history, and your version, and Karl Rove is pretty good at getting people to believe George's version of truth (Moore, 2003; Corn, 2003; Ivins, 2003).

VOICE # 7: AUTHOR:

But people are dying under his version of truth!

VOICE # 8: G. W. BUSH, COMMANDER-IN-CHIEF:

God Bless these brave Americans who die in Iraq. They are protecting us from the terrorists.

VOICE # 9: MARK TWAIN—A WAR PRAYER FOR DUBYA:

George, here is a prayer you can use as you send brave Americans off to battle: 'O Lord our Father, as our young patriots, idols of our hearts, go forth to battle—be Thou near them! With them—in spirit—we also go forth from the sweet peace of our beloved firesides to smite the foe. O Lord our God help us to tear their soldiers to bloody shreds with our shells; help us to cover their smiling fields with the pale forms of their patriot dead; help us to drown the thunder of their guns with the shrieks of their wounded, writhing in pain; help us to lay waste their humble homes with a hurricane of fire; help us to wring the hearts of their unoffending widows with unavailing grief; help us to turn them out roofless with their little children to wander unfriended the wastes of their desolated land in rags and hunger and thirst . . . imploring Thee for the refuge of the grave . . . Lord blast their hopes, blight their lives, protract their bitter pilgrimage . . . We ask it, in the spirit of love, of Him Who is the Source of Love . . . Amen' (Twain, 1963a, p. 682).

VOICE # 10: G. W. BUSH, THE HISTORIAN:

"There are some who would like to rewrite history, but I'm not one of 'em."

"I'm a uniter, not a divider, and I don't believe in nation building."

"We found the weapons of mass destruction"

"If there is a problem with intelligence . . . it doesn't mean that anybody mislead anybody."

"When it's all said and done, the facts will show the world the truth."

"We will, in fact, be greeted as liberators."

"The reason I don't use the phrase 'guerilla war' is because there isn't one."

"There are some people in our country who doubted the Iraqi people wanted freedom."

"First and foremost is to tell the truth."

VOICE # 11: GREGORY ULMER (PARAPHRASING BENJAMIN):

You must read history as catastrophe (Benjamin, 1968, p. 263; Ulmer, 1989, p. 112), as lost opportunity, as a critical moment that could have moved in another direction.

VOICE # 12: MOLLY IVINS AND CARL POPE (PARAPHRASED):

And gosh, George has given us so many opportunities. But there is little to be gained by listing all of his sins, because there are so many of them. For example, we could list the top ten environmental sins of his administration (Pope, 2003, p. 8), including: clear-cutting ancient forests, his multibillion dollar giveaway programs to agribusiness corporations, the pollution of drinking water, the fraudulent Clean Air Proposals, lifting EPA environmental pollution guidelines, the refusal to sign the Kyoto Treaty; or his top 10 education, or welfare, justice, or health care sins (see Ivins, 2003).

VOICE # 13: BELL HOOKS (PARAPHRASED):

To turn Bush's white patriarchal, crony capitalist history back against him means to seize and hold up a series of memories and images and read these images as signs of critical moments where history could have gone in a different direction.

VOICE # 14: DAVID CORN FOR G. W. BUSH, THE REVISIONIST HISTORIAN:

My fellow Americans, there may be threatening amounts of weapons of mass destruction in Iraq. There may not be. We're not sure. The intelligence is not conclusive . . . they could be gone—that is if there were there in the first place . . . After we defeat Iraq's brutal regime, the people of Iraq may welcome U. S. troops as liberators. Then again, within days, many of them could be shouting, 'Yankee, go home' . . . we do not really know of any operational links between Saddam Hussein and al Qaeda (Corn, 2003, pp. 322–323).

VOICE # 15: DOUBTER (DAVID CORN PARAPHRASED):

With such a truthful pitch, would G. W. have persuaded America, the Congress and Tony Blair that war was unavoidable? The answer of course is no. George had to lie to get the war he wanted. Now, can he lie his way out of it?

VOICE # 16: WALTER BENJAMIN ON HISTORY AND PUPPETS:

The story is told of an automaton constructed in such a way that it could play a winning game of chess, answering each move of an opponent with a countermove. A puppet in a Turkish attire and with a hookah in its mouth sat before a chessboard placed on a large table. . a system of mirrors created the illusion that this table was transparent from all sides. Actually, a little hunchback who was an expert chess player sat inside and guided the puppet's hand by means of strings. One can imagine a philosophical counterpart to this device. The puppet called 'historical materialism' is to win all the time. It can easily be a match for anyone if it enlists the services of theology, which today, as we know, is wizened and has to keep out of sight (Benjamin, 1968, p. 255).

Voice # 15: Skeptic:

So who is the puppet and who is the automaton? Who pulls Bush's strings? What happens when this Fascist theology goes public? Can people see it? Can it be lied about? Do people believe that they need to lose their freedom in order to be free? Is freedom more than another name for nothin' left to lose?

VOICE # 16: WALTER BENJAMIN ON EMERGENCIES (PARAPHRASED):

The 'state of emergency' in which we live is not the exception but the rule. We must attain a conception of history that is in keeping with this insight. Then we shall clearly realize that our task is to bring about a real state of emergency, and this will improve our position in the struggle against Fascism.

VOICE # 17: MARK TWAIN:

Yessir, you've got to challenge how the fascists control language. Take the word patriot. Patriotism under fascism is a form of religion, the thoughtless worship of flag and country. The newspaper and politician manufactured Patriot becomes necessary when insane political wars are being created; then men are trained to manufacture thoughtless Patriotism (Twain, 1963c, pp. 567–68).

VOICE # 18: WALTER BENJAMIN:

One reason why Fascism has a chance is that in the name of progress its opponents treat it as a historical norm. The current amazement that the things we are experiencing are 'still' possible in the twenty-first century is not philosophical. This amazement is not the beginning of resistance and rebellion, unless it is understood that the view of history that gives rise to it is untenable and unacceptable (1968, p. 259)!

VOICE # 19: NARRATOR:

I think I want a new puppet master. No, on second thought, I want to be free of puppets and their masters. I want a new philosophical scheme, no more mirrors. I'm tired of a government that misuses the word democracy, rules by creating crises, and rejects nonviolence and negotiation as preferred political strategies.

VOICE # 20: PAULO FREIRE:

You want an ethics of love, a progressive politic that dreams of a new democracy, a serious democracy that reinvents power, is committed to doing justice to everyone, a nonviolent equalitarian democratic state, a politics of hope, love, and freedom (Darder, 2002, pp. 46–47).

VOICE # 21: WALT WHITMAN:

We have frequently printed the word Democracy. Yet I cannot too often repeat that it is a word the real gist of which still sleeps, quite unawaken'd . . . It is great word, whose history, I suppose remains unwritten, because that history has yet too be enacted (1982, p. 960).

VOICE # 22: MOLLY IVINS (PARAPHRASED):

Don't you progressives go and let Dubya and the other Professional Official Fibbers use the word democracy to desribe what they are doing in Iraq! Don't you let that happen. Lets take back this great word and give it a new history.

The End

Note

1. I follow Benjamin's advice about writing history under a fascist regime. Such histories consist of a series of quotations, documents and texts placed side-by-side, producing a de-centered narrative, a multi-voiced text with voices and speakers speaking back and forth, often past one another.

   Benjamin's histories rip the present out of its present context, refusing to privilege the past, for fascism's history only unfolds as a series of interconnected presents, one crisis, one catastrophe, one state of alert, one national emergency seamlessly knitted into the next. Quoting the present back to itself exposes these contradictions and ruptures in the fascist project (Benjamin, 1983, p. 24; 1968, pp. 255–266). The story of Bush's administration has been the story of one crisis after another, starting with 9/11/01, moving then from one war to the next (Corn, 2003).

References

Benjamin, Walter. (1968). *Illuminations*. Trans. Harry Zohn. New York: Harcourt, Brace & World, Inc.

Benjamin, Walter. (1983). N Theoretics of Knowledge: Theory of Progress. *The Philosophical Forum*, 15.

Corn, David. (2003). *The Lies of George W. Bush: Mastering the Politics of Deception*. New York: Crown Publishers.

Darder, Antonia. (2002). *Reinventing Paulo Freire: A Pedagogy of Love*. Boulder, Colorado: Westview Press.

Ivins, Molly with Lou Dubose. (2003). *Bushwacked: Life in Geroge W. Bush's America*. New York: Random House.

Franken, Al. (2003). *Lies (and the Lying Liars Who Tell Them): A Fair and Balanced Look at the Right*. New York: Dutton.

Moore, Michael. (2003). *Dude, Where's My Country*. New York: Warner Books.

New York Times. (2003, November 16). "Editorial: Iraq Goes Sour." Editorials/Letters, p. 12.

Pope, Carl. (2003, November, December). "Big Pigs at the Trough: The Worst Agriculture Policy Money Can Buy." *Sierra*, 88, (8) pp. 8–9.

Ulmer, Gregory. (1989). *Teletheory: Grammatology in the Age of Video*. New York: Routledge.

Stam, Juan. (2003, December 22). Bush's Religious Language. *The Nation*, Vol. 277, (21), p. 27.

Twain, Mark. (1963a). The War Prayer. In *The Complete Essays of Mark Twain*, Edited and with an Introduction by Charles Neider (pp. 679–682). New York: Doubleday (written 1904–05).

Twain, Mark. (1963b). A Word of Encouragement for our Blushing Exiles. In *The Complete Essays of Mark Twain*, Edited and with an Introduction by Charles Neider (pp. 682–684). New York: Doubleday (Written 1898).

Twain, Mark. (1963c). As Regards Patriotism. In *The Complete Essays of Mark Twain*, Edited and with an Introduction by Charles Neider (pp. 566–568). New York: Doubleday (written, 1900).

Whitman, Walt. (1982). Democratic Vistas. In Walt Whitman: *Collected Poetry and Collected Prose*, edited by Justin Kaplan (pp. 929–994). New York: The Library of America (originally published 1867).

Part 3

Life after 11-04-04

10

Homegrown Democracy, Homegrown Democrats[1]

(10-11-04)

Another political story, a narrative about political depression.

We are 45 days out and counting from the 2004 election. Bush is leading Kerry in every national poll. I despair. Nothing is working. Yesterday the *New York Times* devoted the entire Op Ed page to advice for the Kerry campaign. "Get a Message" seemed to be the message, and "stay on it." Fifty percent of the American public think the country is headed in the wrong direction, and Bush is still leading Kerry by 13 points.

The cracks in the history of this administration have been exposed. The Bush Presidency has trashed the environment, welfare, education, the economy, turned the rest of the world against us, and over 10,000 Iraqis and 1000 Americans have died in his dirty little Middle Eastern war. There are more than 100 anti-Bush books, and still counting. Bush's lies have been catalogued, documented and analyzed (Corn, 2003; Dowd, 2004; Ivins, 2003; Moore, 2003; Pope, 2003; Powers, 2003; Alterman and Green, 2004). There were no weapons of mass destruction. The Iraqi do not love us. Bush was warned in advance of bin Ladden's desire to strike the U.S., and sat by doing nothing. And yet none of this seems to matter. Bush's handlers have turned fantasy into reality. Sixty percent of the voters still think Saddam supported Al Qaeda.

Critics assert that George Bush is a liar, a "President who knowingly and deliberately twists facts for political gain" (Hersh, 2004, p. 367; Corn, 2003). Turning intelligence estimates and wishful thinking into statements of fact has become an art form in this administration. Even Karl Rove knew, if Bush did not, that arguments about Saddam's WMD program were based on "estimates full of judgments, not absolute certainties" (Woodward, 2004, p. 219). Indeed, Rove understands the difference between a fact and intelligence. Paraphrasing Woodward, "If it's a fact, is not called intelligence." (Woodward, 2004, p. 219).

But to call Bush a liar assumes that his lying indicates "an understanding of what is desired, what is possible, and how best to get there. A more plausible explanation is that words have no meaning for this President beyond the immediate moment, and so he believes that his mere utterance of the phrases makes them real. It is a terrifying possibility" (Hersh, 2004, p. 367). Indeed!

* * *

The discourse about Bush's lying presumes that there is reality against which assertions of truth and lying can be judged. This is a contested assertion. In the postmodern age of simulation, the hypperreal is more real than the real. Baudrillard (1983) taught us this. In such a regime, a lie is true if it conforms to the hypperreal; that is, if it has the appearance of truth. Bush and his handlers skillfully manipulate this postmodern logic, insuring that his assertions about the real have the appearance of being truthful. Indeed the entire Iraqi War was premised on this model.

The public was sold the belief that WMDs existed in an empirical reality. The inspectors would be able to locate the weapons, even though Saddam claimed they did not exist. Indeed, Saddam's lies proved the weapons existed. In the end the weapons did not need to found. Their absence meant they existed. We had no choice but to go to war.

The media model that scripted Bush's war short-circuited history by manipulating the logic of the hypperreal. It created instant meaning by producing a fictional sense of public opinion which supported the war. Saddam and Al Queda were connected. Saddam was evil. Al Queda is evil. The war was making America safer from terrorists. A total mythological system was in place. A closed system where lies became truth, and truth became that which conformed to the hypperreal. And this is how we got into this mess.

Any attempt to check-mate this system by remaining within this structural communication grid is doomed to failure. Three thousand books proving that

Bush is a liar will not alter the fact that we are in this war. The discourse about lies and truth is a dead-end.

* * *

In the face of all of this I turn to Arundhati Roy for wisdom and understanding. She speaks for me (2004, p. 41). We are living in a time of "Instant-Mix Imperial Democracy (bring to a boil, add oil, then bomb)" (2004. p. 47). We are, "the people of the world, confronted with an Empire armed with a mandate from heaven . . . an Empire that has conferred upon itself the right to go to war at will and the right to deliver people from corrupting ideologies . . . by the age-old, tried-and-tested practice of extermination" (2004, p. 47).

This Empire cannot stand still. It "is on the move, and Democracy is its sly new war cry. Democracy, home-delivered to your doorstep, by daisy-cutters. Death is a small price for people to pay for the privilege of sampling this new product: Instant-Mix Imperial Democracy" (2004. p. 47).

Like many, I too am tired of " racing to keep abreast of the speed at which our freedoms are being snatched from us" (Roy, 2004, p. 41). Who among us "can afford the luxury of retreating from the streets for a while in order to return with an exquisite, fully formed political thesis" (Roy, 2004, p. 41)? Apparently neither John Kerry nor the Democratic party.

* * *

And so I felt a great excitement when I saw Garrison Keillor's new book, *Homegrown Democrat* (2004). I thought, here is a man who thinks deeply about democracy, and these troubling times we are living in. He'll pull me out of my depression. So I bought the book.

Keillor occupies a special place in my biography. Without fail, every Saturday at 5:00 p. m. I listen to *A Prairie Home Companion*. I love the folk music, and the jazz, Guy Noir, the stories from Lake Wobegon, the opening monologues, which have for the last four years frequently mocked George Bush. I love Keillor's 1960's sensibilities, his mid-life struggles with fatherhood, his wry humor, his efforts to find a comfortable place inside this neoconservative project called corporate globalization. I love his criticisms of the neoconservatives, how they have molded the instruments of democracy, including an independent judiciary, a free press, and the right to vote to their own purposes (Roy, 2004, p. 3).

So I fixed a glass of iced tea, grabbed *Homegrown Democracy* and settled into a comfortable chair on my deck, basking in the late afternoon sun. Time for a little Lake Wobegon therapy. What is this thing Keillor calls homegrown democracy? It is surely not anything like Bush's "Instant-Mix Imperial Democracy," that home-delivered democracy that arrives with a war cry and a bomb.

To my delight, I felt right at home. Keillor dedicates his book "to all of the good democratic-farmer laborites of Minnesota" (p. x). These are my people, farmers from the heartland. Democrats.

Homegrown Democracy moves in three directions at the same time. It is a short version of Keillor's autobiography. It is his attack on Bush, the Iraqi war, the neo-cons, and conservative Republicans. It is his celebration of the values mean-spirited Republicans, corporate shills, hobby cops, misanthropic frat boys, and gun fetishists have attacked. These are the homegrown democratic values of the hard-working, God-fearing people of Lake Wobegon, and their idea of the common good.

The Republicans have broken the civic compact, the simple code of the Golden Rule that underlies Midwestern civility. The politics of kindness. The obligation to defend the weak against the powerful. "I didn't become a Democrat because I was angry" (p. 58), he writes. "I'm a Democrat because I received a good education in the public schools of Anoka, Minnesota, and attended a great university and when I was 18, John F. Kennedy ran for president."

This is my story! I attended excellent public schools in Iowa City, Iowa. I attended a great university, the University of Iowa. And, much to the ire of my Republican grandfather, I voted for John F. Kennedy for president. Like Keillor, I worked to put myself through college. I discovered classical music, lecture halls, libraries, concerts, plays, opera, modern art, jazz, Dave Brubeck, great books, Sociology, classic literature, professors who cared about teaching, all-night cafes, coffee shops, existentialism, Marxism, Sartre, Camus, Hemingway, C. Wright Mills, folk music, the civil rights and anti-war movements.

I paid $93 for a semester's tuition and soon found my way to the long reading tables in the University Library. Around me, as there were for Keillor, were young men and women like myself, "bent to the hard work of scholarship, folks for whom attending college was not an assumed privilege" (Keillor, 2004, p. 63).

We dressed alike, ate the same food, listened to the same juke box music in the small cafes. We'd come early, before 7:00 p. m. to get a good table, my friends and I. And there we would sit, books stacked in front of us, sharpened pencils, heads bowed, "rows and rows of us, reading, reading, reading—sons of garage mechanics on their way to medical school, daughters of dairy farmers out to become professors of Romance languages" (pp. 63–64).

In the Music Room in the Iowa Memorial Union I discovered Ravel's "Bolareo" and learned how to smoke a pipe and look existential, and read philosophy. There I sat, in my favorite chair, lost in the music, looking to others to see how to do this. We had a purpose, a sense of vocation, we could have stepped out of Thomas Hart Benton's great mural, "The Children of the Great Plains Claiming Their Birthright." We were "taking our once-in-a-lifetime chance to realize our God-given talent . . . no guarantees of success" (Keillor, 2004, pp. 64–65), hard work, a love of this life, reading, reading, reading, reading.

I moved back into this space as I turned the pages of *Homegrown Democrat*. I shared my warm feelings of nostalgia with Aisha Durham, who reminded me that this sounded a lot like a white man' story about college in the 1950s. She asked, "Were there any African-American's in that music room?" Stunned, I searched back in my memory. There were no African-Americans in Iowa City, well, one family. There was a black man on the basketball team for a while but they sent him back to New York City for gambling. Aisha was right.

I went back to Keillor too see what he said about race. Democrats, he states, "have changed American in simple basic ways in the past fifty years that have benefited everyone. Race has become less and less an issue in people's lives and racism has ceased to be socially acceptable anywhere. Women have moved into every realm of society . . . Equal opportunity in education, employment, housing . . . Homegrown Democrats led the way in bringing these things about" (p. 26). Indeed!

I can't let these lines stand without protest. In my community racism is on the rise. We have more, not less discrimination. Hate crimes are a daily occurrence. Women have hit glass ceilings, and the community drove our last Chancellor out of town. They said she was insensitive to local tradition, the "Chief Mascot." Maybe we don't have the right kind of Democrat in Urbana. I doubt it.

In the chapter"The Good Democrat," he lists ten characteristics of Democrats. Democrats distrust privilege and power (p. 169); regard equality as bedrock (p. 172); are inclusive and integrationist to the core (p. 174); are city people at heart . . . The city is the crowning achievement of society (p. 176); believe in individualism (p. 180); are union guys (p. 182); have sympathy for the helpless, especially children and the elderly (p. 185); are diehard teachers (p.

189); are realists (p. 192); have values that are rooted in courtesy and kindness (p. 195). The good Democrat is homegrown, from the great Midwestern heartland, the land of Lake Wobegons.

The last chapter addresses 9/11, reading it as a rare moment of shared community, pain and suffering in New York City. Anticipating the Republican National Convention, which celebrated Bush and 9/11, Keillor invokes the men and women who died that day, "They deserve better than to be the platform for intolerance" (p. 232).

He catches himself. "I refuse to be furious. I am a happy Democrat living in a great country, at home in St. Paul, Minnesota, where no matter what, there is a lot of satisfaction going on a good deal of the time" (p. 233).

* * *

I'm an angry Democrat. I'm angry at the Democrats who supported Bush's war. I'm angry at politicians who wait to see which way the wind is blowing before they commit a political act requiring honesty and courage. I'm tired of Democrats who make lists. I'm angry at Democrats who think the good Democrat is homegrown. I'm not sure homegrown works any longer; my homegrown was narrow and provincial, and white. In my Lake Wobegon the Golden Rule and the politics of kindness, and the obligation to defend the weak and the poor only extended to those folks like the rest of us.

I agree we have a moral obligation to bequeath this world to our grandchildren in better shape than we found it. But it is not just our grandchildren to whom this world is bequeathed. This is a global project. I know it must be local, but I do not think it can be entirely built from the values that circulate in Keillor's imaginary pastoral utopia. And this saddens me because for a long time I time I have liked going to Lake Wobegon at the end of a hard week. I'm not so sure I can any longer do this.

I must look elsewhere for my alternative model of democracy.

Note

1. I thank Michael Giardina and Jack Bratich for their comments on an earlier draft of this manuscript.

References

Alterman, Eric, and Mark Green. (2004). *The Book on Bush: How George W. (Mis)leads America.* New York: Penguin Books.

Baudrillard, Jean. (1983). *Simulations.* New York: Semiotext (3).

Corn, David. (2003). *The Lies of George W. Bush: Mastering the Politics of Deception.* New York: Crown Publishers.

Dowd, Maureen. (2004). *Bushworld.: Enter at your Own Risk.* New York: G. P. Putnam's Sons.

Hersh, Seymour M. (2004). *Chain of Command: The Road from 9/11 to Abu Ghraib.* New York: HarperCollins.

Ivins, Molly with Lou Dubose. (2003). *Bushwacked: Life in Geroge W. Bush's America.* New York: Random House.

Keillor, Garrison. (2004). *Homegrown Democrat: A Few Plain thoughts for the Heart of America.* New York: Viking.

Moore, Michael. (2003). *Dude, Where's My Country.* New York: Warner Books.

Pope, Carl. (2003, November, December). "Big Pigs at the Trough: The Worst Agriculture Policy Money Can Buy." *Sierra*, 88, (8), pp. 8–9.

Powers, Thomas. (2003. December 4). "The Vanishing Case for War." *The New York Review of Books*, 50, (19), pp. 12–17

Roy, Arundhati. (2004). *An Ordinary Person's Guide to Empire.* Cambridge, Mass.: South End Press.

Woodward, Bob. (2004). *Plan of Attack.* New York: Simon & Schuster.

11

After the Election: Surviving Bush's Democracy[1]

(3-22-05)

Written six months after the 2004 American Presidential election, this political narrative asks if democracy can survive under the Bush regime.

A narrative about political depression, life after the 2004 American Presidential election. We are six months into the second Bush Administration. Liberals and progressives despair. Bush is committed to eviscerating Medicare, and to dismantling Social Security, one of the last vestiges of New Deal Democracy (Krugman, 2004, p. A27). Using a faith-based model of science, Bush seems determined to remove all barriers separating church and state.

It is impossible to say anything new about this administration. It has trashed the environment, welfare, education, the economy. It has turned the rest of the world against us, and over 10,000 Iraqis and 1500 Americans have died in the illegal occupation of Iraq. Fifty percent of the American public think the country is headed in the wrong direction.

Meanwhile, this administration takes to a new level the meaning of the staged news event. The White House borrows its techniques of news management from Jon Stewart, host of the "Daily Show." Fake newsmen, looking like real newsmen, use the techniques of real news programs to deliver fake news in prime time (Rich, 2005a, p. 20). The use of fake reporters—six and counting—producing fake news stories has been exposed. The administration paid $240,000 to Armstrong Williams for delivering "faux-journalistic analyses of the No Child Left Behind Act" (Rich, 2005b, p. 8).

Bush's handlers script "town hall" meetings. The Pentagon Office of Strategic Information asserts that Iraqis attacked the U. S. on 9/11. The President assures the public and the world that the deplorable crimes of Abu Ghraib were not condoned at the highest levels but rather the result of but a few ill-trained soldiers. Under Bush a lie is true if it has the appearance of truth. Through the use of fake reporters, the creation of phantom publics, and the production of moral crises connected to imagined new terrorist attacks, the regime creates instant support for its initiatives. Manipulating the logic of the lie that looks like the truth, Bush's handlers insure that his assertions about the real have the appearance of being truthful.

* * *

And so the perpetual war on terror must continue because terrorists oppose freedom and truth. Terrorists hate democracy. Every person has the God-given right to freedom and to life under a democratic state. Indeed freedom can only happen under democracy. Therefore America's battle for democracy in the Middle East is making America (and the world) safe from terrorists. By bringing freedom to the Middle East, we attack the terrorists who would destroy democracy in the name of false political ideals. The Bush administration has created a closed ideological system, a system that is violent to the core. Attempts to check-mate this system are doomed to failure if the critic remains within the systems structural grid.

* * *

Arundhati Roy is right. Under Bush we are living in a time of "Instant-Mix Imperial Democracy" (2004. p. 47). Imperial Democracy forces its will on the people. This is not grassroots, participatory democracy. This is not Walt Whitman's wild, radical democracy. This is not a democracy that sings through the body-politic (Whitman, 1993). It is not a democracy that is bone-deep in the moral landscape and soul of a people (Mailer, 2003, p. 52). Imperial democracy is totalitarian fascism masquerading as Democracy. Imperial democracy is state-sponsored violence masquerading as Democracy. Democracy is its new war cry (Roy, 2004, p. 7). We may not survive Bush Democracy.

* * *

A truly vital and revolutionary democracy lives in the free open spaces of a society. Democracy is open-ended. It is a set of ideals that are decidedly non-partisan: commitments to non-violence, preservation of the environment, economic justice, civil rights, a just educational and health care system, humane foreign policy, human rights, freedom, a decent life for all (Springsteen, 2004, p. A24). Democracy lives in nature, in the 'natural' environments that we inhabit, in those sacred, moral spaces where we take a stance, where we become citizens of a place, a landscape, a city, a nation, of the world (Lane-Zucker, 2004, p. ii).

Democracy-as-citizenship is radically performative, dialogical, transgressive, pedagogical. It is poetry in motion. It is a dance, it is sunlight at mid-day dancing off of a flowing river, it is a rainbow painted across a blue sky, it is a performance embodying reflective activism, a never-ending project, a world without end. Perhaps we can survive Bush Democracy afterall (Glover and Fletcher, 2005, p. 22).

* * *

Note

1. I thank Michael Giardina for his comments on an earlier version of this manuscript.

References

Glover, Danny, and Bill Fletcher Jr. (2005, February 14). "Visualizing a Neo-Rainbow." *The Nation*, Vol. 280, (6), pp. 19–22.

Krugman. Paul. (2004, November 5). No Surrender. *New York Times*, Op Ed. p. A27.

Lane-Zucker, Laurie. (2004). "Foreword," In Terry Tempest Williams. *The Open Spaces of Democracy*, pp. i–iii. Great Barrington, Mass: The Orion Society.

Mailer, Norman. (2003, March 27). "Only in America." *New York Review of Books*, 50, (5), pp. 49–53.

Rich, Frank. (2005a, February 20). The White House Stages Its 'Daily Show.' *New York Times*, Arts & Leisure, Section 2, pp. 1, 20.

Rich, Frank. (2005b, March 20). "Enron: Patron Saint of Bush's Fake News."" *New York Times*, Arts & Leisure, Section 2. pp. 1, 8.

Roy, Arundhati. (2004). *An Ordinary Person's Guide to Empire.* Cambridge, Mass.: South End Press.

Springsteen, Bruce. (2004, August 5). "Chords of Change." *New York Times*, p. A24.

Williams, Terry Tempest. (2004). *The Open Spaces of Democracy.* Great Barrington, Mass: The Orion Society.

Whitman, Walt. (1993). *Leaves of Grass and Selected Prose.* London: J. M. Dent, Orion Publishing Company.

12

Science Under Bush: A Call to Arms[1]

(9-1-05)

It is now clear that science has been politicized by the Bush administration and the far-right. Under George W. Bush, the White House has treated science "as a nuisance, and scientists as an interest group—one that, because it lies outside the governing conservative coalition—need not be indulged" (Hertzberg, 2005, p. 22). Whether in the service of multinational corporations, warring neo-conservatives, or the far-right conservative Christian coalition, the White House has used science to its own ends (Lather, 2004; Lincoln and Cannella, 2004). These practices by the far-right to redefine science in religious terms must be resisted. They cannot be allowed to take science and its methodologies away from the scientific community. They cannot be allowed to treat science as if it were a handmaiden of religion.

Indeed, according to the Union for Concerned Scientists (Anderson, 2004; quoted on Kaplan, 2005, p. 128), "There is significant evidence that the scope and scale of the manipulation, suppression, and misrepresentation of science by the Bush administration is unprecedented." The administration ignores and distorts those findings of science that contradict the moral positions of the religious right. In the name of pseudo, fake, or junk science, it manufactures evidence to support its positions (Kaplan, 2005, p. 95).

The list is long. This administration has altered, suppressed, and overridden "scientific warnings on global warming; missile defense; HIV/AIDS; pollution from industrial farming and oil drilling; forest management and endangered species; environmental health, including lead and mercury poisoning in children and safety standards for drinking water; and non-abstinence methods of birth control" (Hertzberg, 2005, p. 22).

It has misled the public on the number of "stem-cell lines that can be used for research" (Hertzberg, 2005, p. 22). It has appointed unqualified persons to scientific advisory committees; fired whistle-blowing scientists; erased large national data files that contradict official White House policy (Kaplan, 2004, p. 96); and hired fake journalists to promote its educational policies (Rich, 2005a, b).

It openly endorses Creationist, or Intelligent Design (ID), explanations of evolution.[2] It discredits biological theories of human evolution, preferring instead a faith-based understanding of science. Indeed, a defeated amendment to the No Child Left Behind legislation of 2001 asserted that creationism should be taught in schools: "Where biological evolution is taught, the curriculum should help students to understand why this subject generates so much continuing controversy" (Wilgoren, 2005, p. 14). The only controversy, however, is generated by fundamentalist adherents to ID.

The Bush Administration has also misled the public on the reasons for going to war against Iraq. "Intelligence and facts were . . . fixed around a policy" (Manning, 2005) justifying military action. The White House manufactured evidence connecting Saddam Hussein with the attacks of 9/11/01, while linking Saddam to al Qaeda, and offering made-up evidence concerning Hussein's probable use of weapons of mass destruction (Corn, 2003, p. 240). Once weapons of mass destruction were not found, Bush shifted the causes and justifications of the war to the need to liberate and bring democracy to Iraq, to protect human rights, to defend the will of the world community and to fight terrorists before they attacked the homeland (Alterman and Green, 2004, p. 284).

Under the auspices of the 2001 No Child Left Behind Act, the Bush Administration has stated that traditional scientific methods are inadequate for purposes of educational reform. It has endorsed evidence-based models of inquiry, which many regard as inappropriate to human subject research, and nearly impossible to implement in concrete research settings (Ryan and Hood, 2004). The result is that schools that do not meet federal standards cannot get federal funding; such funding, though, can be directed to charter schools or parochial schools that can discriminate.

At the same time, under the guise of endorsing Intelligent Design (see below), the Administration has launched a full-scale attack on the logic and methods of modern science. Thus, while they have raised the bar concerning the standards for conducting and evaluating educational research, they have similarly moved to debunk these same standards in other areas. This allows them to have it both ways. Modern science cannot get us to where we want to be in our schools, and we will use the methods of science to prove the case!

The Wedge Document: Seeing the Forest, and not the Trees

The Bush attacks on and mis uses of science fit into a larger pattern; namely the use of deception and lies to gain and maintain power. More deeply, Bush's agenda has helped advance the goals of his three major constituencies: the religious right, big business, and neoconservatives (Alterman and Green, 2004). The interests of these three groups coalesce into a larger political agenda—the systematic destruction of the progressive political gains of the last century (Alterman and Green, 2004).

In order to turn back the clock, the far right had to politicize and redefine science. If science can be undone, or debunked, its findings can no longer be used by liberals and progressives to advance the goals of social justice, and the Great Society initiatives of the last century. Science had to be redefined from within a religious, faith-based framework. Intelligent Design works toward doing just this. It advocates a theistic, faith-based model of science. The attacks on conventional science, including biology and evolutionary theory, are pivotal to the goals of far right Christian fundamentalists, who were waging a war on science even before the 2000 election (Mooney, 2005; Kaplan, 2004).

* * *

There are various origin stories of ID. One starts in the 1960s with Barry Goldwater and his anti-civil rights presidential campaign. Another starting point is 1990 and the founding of the conservative Discovery Institute, which has been called "the institutional love child of Ayn Rand and Jerry Falwell" (Wilgoren, 2005, p.14). Named after the H. M. S. Discovery which explored Puget Sound in 1792 (Wilgoren, 2005, p. 14), the Institute, and its Center for Science & Culture, has financial support from the Verizon Foundation, the Gates Foundation, and the Henry P. and Susan G. Crowell Trust (whose mission is the "teaching and active extension of the doctrines of evangelical Christianity") (Wilgoren, 2005, p. 14). The goals of the institute are contained in an internal memorandum known as the Wedge Document.

The Institute is ostensibly concerned only with science, and with advancing the belief that the universe was created through an act of "intelligent design." However, its intentions, as spelled out in the Wedge Document, go beyond criticisms of Darwin and modern evolutionary theory. Its bedrock assumption holds that human beings are created in the image of God. According to the Institute, our entire Western civilization is built on this assumption. As we know, 19th century intellectuals and thinkers as diverse as Darwin, Freud, and Marx, drawing on the discoveries of modern science, started to debunk traditional conceptions of man and God. These thinkers portrayed human beings as animals or machines who lived in a universe ruled by the forces of biology, chemistry and physics. ID ideologues, however, believe this materialist conception of reality eventually "infected every area of our culture, from politics and economics to literature and art" (Wedge Document, p. 1).

According to this Wedge Document, which outlines a five- and twenty-year strategic plan aimed at defeating scientific materialism, the Institute "seeks nothing less than the overthrow of materialism and its cultural legacies" (p. 1). Bringing together so-called leading scholars from the natural and social sciences, and the humanities, the Institute "explores how new developments in biology, physics, and cognitive science raise serious doubts about scientific materialism and have re-opened the case for a broadly theistic understanding of nature" (Wedge Document, p. 1). This broadly theistic, non-materialist conception of nature, culture and society is foundational. It underwrites a conservative model of the modern nation-state. In its most aggressive form it authorizes wars and global struggles against America's enemies, including terrorists and violent extremists.

The document argues, and I quote at length:

> If we view the predominant materialistic science as a giant tree, our strategy is intended to function as a 'wedge' that while effectively small, can split the trunk when applied to its weakest point . . . We are broadening the wedge with a positive scientific alternative to materialistic scientific theories, which has come to be called the theory of intelligent design (IDT). Design Theory promises to reverse the stifling dominance of the materialist worldview, and to replace it with a science consonant with Christian theistic convictions . . . with the theistic understanding that nature and human beings are created by god (Wedge Document, pp. 3–4).

Yet nowhere in the document is a Christian theistic model of science presented. Further, all that makes ID a positive scientific alternative is the claim that it rejects the discoveries of modern science. This would seemingly make it a negative—not a positive—"scientific" alternative.

The Wedge strategy is divided into three phases: research, writing, and publication; publicity and opinion-making; cultural confrontation and renewal. The documents offers an extensive bibliography of books written by ID advocates, a listing of journals where academic articles have appeared, television and radio appearances, and newspaper and magazine articles. Immediate and long-term goals and objectives of the Institute include: having ID accepted as the dominant perspective in molecular biology, biochemistry, paleontology, physics, psychology, ethics, and the fine arts; staging major public debates between "design theorists" and Darwinists; securing regular press coverage on new developments in design "theory"[3]; convincing the major Christian denominations that they should defend the doctrines of ID; having at least 10 states include ID in their required curriculum; and funding two universities where ID is the dominant view.

Whose Science and Science for Whom?

Much is at stake with ID and its ideological underpinnings. It threatens every sphere of contemporary life. It threatens to undermine not only our schools and universities, but the environment, our welfare and legal systems, modern medicine, the institutions and disciplines of modern science, contemporary systems of philosophy and ethics. If these institutions can be discredited, then the very foundation of democracy, which requires a separation between church and state, disappears. America becomes a theocracy ruled by the divine visions of the Christian right who claim God is on their side.

In attacking modern science, and in preserving the myth of a separate divine creation, the movement displays a fearful self-righteousness, an arrogance, and a destructive hubris (Klinkenborg, 2005). It wishes to "set us apart from nature, except to dominate it. It misses both the grace and the moral depth of knowing that humans have only the same stake . . . in the Earth as every living creature that has ever lived" (Klinkenborg, 2005).

It has no methodology, other than the vague notion of a "faith-based science." It is a way to bring the values of conservative religious ideology into the classroom. To date ID has produced no scientific experiments to challenge mainstream biology. It has offered no "observations from the fossil record . . . or comparative anatomy that undermine standard evolutionary thinking" (Dennett, 2005). No testable hypotheses derived from ID have ever been offered. Indeed there is no content to the "theory" that can be tested. "Since there is no content, there is 'no controversy' to teach about in biology class" (Dennett, 2005).

In arguing for faith over evidence, it opens the door for misrepresentations of reality. Misrepresentation is part and parcel of Bush's politics. His handlers script town meetings, call defeats major victories, and make every lie look like a fact. This gives each Bush lie the feeling of a bad dream experienced before. Misrepresentation is basic to the ID approach to reality.

Like Bush, Intelligent Design ideologues ignore the fact that "evolution is a robust theory, in the scientific sense, that has been tested and confirmed again and again" (Klinkenborg, 2005). Then again, ID has no method for testing a theory. To put it ever so bluntly, Intelligent Design "is not a theory, as scientists understand the word, but a well-financed political and religious campaign to muddy science" (Klinkenborg, 2005). Their basic proposition—the intervention of a designer, a.k.a. God—cannot be tested. It has no evidence to offer, and its assumptions that humans were divinely created are the same as its conclusions (Klinkenborg, 2005).

If ID has no content, then there can be no argument for teaching it in the schools. But listen to Dennett, who suggests that what might taught is the question, "Is intelligent design a hoax? And, if so, how was it perpetuated?" (Dennett, 2005). Hoaxes are one thing, some can even be benign. But this is not the case for the hoaxes associated with ID and with Bush. People are dying because of their lies and misrepresentation. How much longer will good people allow this to happen?

In Conclusion: A Call To Arms

However dangerous the assault on science is under the Bush regime, there is more at stake than the individual acts of teaching Intelligent Design in schools, implementing partisan political legislation such as No Child Left Behind, ransacking environmental controls, misinforming the public and spreading misinformation about science, and fostering breeches between science, the government, and democracy. Rather, what these moves collectively reveal is that ***Bush and his neo-conservative supporters want to undo contemporary culture as it is currently understood.***

To repeat, when scientific knowledge and the facts of the real world contradict its political goals, the Bush administration, paraphrasing Kaplan (2005, p. 95), and Anderson (2004), manipulates the process by which science and empirical reality enter into its decisions. It censors research on AIDS, birth control, abortion, and cancer. If scientists recommend polices that challenge right-wing beliefs, the policies will not be implemented. It stacks scientific review panels with "believers who filter data through a religious prism" (Kaplan, 2005, p. 96).

Leading scientists, and scholarly associations including more than 60 Nobel Prize winners, medical science researchers, and the American Sociological Association, have all spoken out against these abuses of science (Kaplan, 2005, pp. 95, 104, 113). The hallmark of a free society is its unfettered support of research and inquiry on ethically and politically sensitive, controversial topics. Such research yields trustworthy findings that many, including those in political power, may find objectionable. But a society's respect for critical interpretive inquiry is "based on the common understanding that serious health, economic, and social consequences are at stake" (Hillman, 2003), not public relations campaigns waged for partisan political gains and the appeasement of far-right religious conservatives.

Safe guards protecting scientists and the scientific community from censorship, misrepresentation, repression, and politicization must be established and enforced. Journalists must understand that balanced coverage of scientific controversies often means giving "equal treatment for fringe or widely discredited views" (Mooney, 2005, p. 253). Scientists must contest anti-environmental politics and "counter creationist efforts at the local level" (Mooney, 2005, p. 255). The values of progressive democracy must be forefront when scientific advice is used for policymaking decisions. The pragmatic consequences for a radical democracy must be taken into account when scientific recommendations for social action are implemented. It is time for all concerned scholars and citizens to rally against the mis-uses of science by the Bush administration and the anti-science right wing of the Republican Party (Mooney, 2005, p. 255).

Notes

1. I thank Michael Giardina for his comments and suggestions.
2. In August of 2005 President Bush, quoted in Dennett(2005) announced that he was in favor of teaching about "intelligent design because I think that part of education is

to expose people to different schools of thought." Senator Bill Frist agreed, "I think in a pluralistic society that is the fairest way to go about education" (Dennett, 2005).

3. The movement is successful in this regard. In August of 2005 the *New York Times* Wilgoren, 2005) the *New Yorker* (Hertzberg) and *Time* magazine ; (Klinkenborg, 2005, all carried major stories about Intelligent Design Theory.

References

Alterman, Eric, and Mark Green. (2004). *The Book on Bush: How George W. (Mis)leads America.* New York: Viking.

Anderson, Philip W. (2004, February 18). Restoring Scientific Integrity to Policymaking, on behalf of the Union for Concerned Scientists, available at www.ucusa.org/global_environment/rst/page.cfm?pageID=1320.

Corn, David. (2003). *The Lies of George W. Bush: Mastering the Politics of Deception.* New York: Crown Publishers.

Dennett, Daniel C. (2005, August 28). Show Me the Science. *New York Times,* Op-Ed, p. 11.

Discovery Institute. (1999). *The Wedge Document.* Seattle: Center for Science and Culture (http://geocities. com/Cappe Canaeral/Hangar/2437/wedge. html) (To be cited as Wedge Document).

Hertzberg, Hendrik. (2005, August 22). Bush Science. *The New Yorker,* pp. 21–22.

Hillman, Sally T. (2003, November 3). "NIH Funded Research and the Peer-Review Process."American Sociological Association Press Release.

Kaplan, Esther. 2005. *With God on Their Side: How Christian Fundamentalists Trampled Science, Policy, and Democracy in the George Bush's White House.* New York: The New Press.

Klinkenborg, Verlyn. (2005, August 23). Grasping the Depth of Time as a First Step in Understanding Evolution. *New York Times,* p. A22.

Lather, Patti. (2004). "This is Your Father's Paradigm: Government Intrusion and the Case of Qualitative Research in Education." *Qualitative Inquiry,* 10 (1), pp. 18–34.

Lincoln, Yvonna, and Gaile S. Cannella. (2004). Dangerous Discourses: Methodological Conservatism and Governmental Regimes of Truth. *Qualitative Inquiry,* 10 (1), pp. 5–10.

Manning, David. (2005, May 1). The Secret Downing Street Memo. *Times online.*

Mooney, Chris. (2005). *The Republican War on Science.* New York: Basic Books.

Rich, Frank. (2005a, February 20). The White House Stages Its 'Daily Show.' *New York Times,* Arts & Leisure, Section 2, pp. 1, 20.

Rich, Frank. (2005b, March 20). Enron: Patron Saint of Bush's Fake News. *New York Times,* Arts & Leisure, Section 2, pp. 1, 8.

Ryan, Katherine, and Lisa K. Hood. (2004). Guarding the Castle and Opening the Gates. *Qualitative Inquiry,* 10 (1), pp. 79–96.

Wilgoren, Jodi. (2005, August 21). Politicized Scholars Put Evolution on the Defensive. The *New York Times,* pp. 1, 14.

13

Katrina and the Collapse of Civil Society in New Orleans[1]

(10-10-05)

> "I don't want to abolish government. I simply want to reduce it to the size where I can drag it into the bathroom and drown it in the bathtub"
> (GROVER NORQUIST, IN FRIEDMAN, 2005).

America's collective relationship to itself, to the Bush Administration, and to the world changed again as a result of the events following Hurricane Katrina.[2] If 9/11/01 and the Iraq War bookend one cataclysmic phase of the Bush Administration, then Katrina marks an equally critical moment. Instead of a single flash-point moment (Johnson[a], 2005, p. 25), the fallout and aftermath of Katrina has unfolded in an infinite series of events and blurred images, including President Bush looking down on the submerged city out of a window from Air Force One.

* * *

> We do not have an exact human vocabulary for the loss of our great iconic city, so graceful . . . insular . . . the one New Orleanians always said that care forgot, and that sometimes . . . forgot to care (Ford, 2005).

* * *

Gloria Ladson-Billings (2003): "They sold slaves in this city. They made a tourist stop out the place where they sold slaves!"

* * *

Constantine, Erickson and Tse (2005: A13): **Areas of New Orleans with significant flooding**: Black (76%); White (18%)

* * *

Hurricane Katrina reduced civil society as it had been known in New Orleans to a size where it was dragged into a huge sinking, stinking outdoor bathroom sometimes called the Big Easy. The erasure of the barriers between the lake, the river, and the city symbolically and materially represented the collapse of the civic structure of the city, and the disappearance of all that we want a humane society to mean for blacks and the urban poor. And the whole world watched in horror.

* * *

There is a clear need for a national conversation on the meanings of the aftermath of Katrina. This tragedy offers an opportunity to rethink what a caring, radically free democratic city might look like. Can we build cities that do not hide racism and poverty behind the facades of culture, cuisine, and carnival? Can we include in the reconstruction of New Orleans the full range of voices that extend across the race, class, and gender spectrum?

* * *

Fragments: A Montage

The Corpse on Union Street

* 7 September 2005: On Union Street in downtown New Orleans a corpse in a body bag decomposes for days, like carrion (Barry, 2005, p. A19).

Meanwhile, the same day,

* Soldiers aims guns at the heads of several men suspected of robbing an electronic store, and a man in a **car** drives by asking for directions

to the interstate (Barry, 2005, pp. A1, A19).
* Mayor to holdouts: "Get out," (*The News Gazette*, Headline, 7 September, 2005, p. 1).
* "45 Bodies found in New Orleans Hospital," (Johnson[b], 2005).

ANNE RICE:

Thousands didn't leave New Orleans because they couldn't leave. They are the poor, black and white . . . To my country I want to say this: During this crisis you failed us; you dismissed our victims . . . You want our Jazz Fest, you want our Mardis Gras, you want our cooking and our music. Then when you saw us in real trouble . . . you turned your back on us (Rice, 2005).

NETANYA WATTS HART:

We walked out of the North Ward in about five feet of water, and we put all the children in a flatboat along with a woman with one leg and walked a mile in the water. Then the water went down enough and we walked about two more miles and all the children were holding hands, singing gospel songs two by two (quoted in Johnson, 2005, p. 32).

BILL O'REILLY, FOX NEWS CHANNEL (ON LOOTING AFTER THE STORM):

A lot of people who stayed wanted to do this destruction, why weren't they being shot on sight? (quoted in Alterman, 2005, p. 11).

BARBARA BUSH (TOURING HURRICANE RELIEF CENTERS IN HOUSTON):

Things are working out very well for the poor evacuees from New Orleans. What I'm hearing is they all want to stay in Texas. Everyone is so overwhelmed by the hospitality. And so many of the people in the arena here, you know, were underprivileged anyway so this—this (chuckles slightly) is working very well for them (2005).

NARRATOR:

I have a color photograph taken in 1973 of my daughters and my father on the upper deck of a large tug boat on the Mississippi River. Jackson Square and Cafe Du Monde are in the background. A black jazz band is playing on the river's edge. My father was the captain on this boat and my daughters were 7 and 8 years old. The wind off the river is blowing their hair. My father has a big grin on his face. The muddy water of the Mississippi River surrounds the boat. There is a smell of rain in the air. A screeching sea gull perches on the boat railing, an orange sun fills the sky.

My father died in 1995. Last week Jackson Square and Cafe Du Monde were under water. The tug boat is long gone. My daughters have faded memories of this trip, remembering the split lip one of them got when grandpa's car was hit by a speeding car in Audubon Park, which was also under water last week.

Today these memories fade into one another, replaced by this scene. The date is 16 August 1977:

> I was in the patio of a live jazz bar on Bourbon Street in the French Quarter the day Elvis Presley died. Six black teenagers sat around a table shucking freshly boiled shrimp. The jazz music stopped and over the loud speakers came the announcement that Elvis had died. The six young men stood up and cheered.

The King of rock and roll was dead, and in New Orleans, in a back patio of a jazz bar, six representatives of black America cheered. This is all I need to know today about race in America. There are two Americas: one black, brown, poor, and disenfranchised; the other white, and propertied, and entertained by the likes of an over the hill white rock and roll singer, who stole his music from blacks.

* * *

Needed: Democratic Reconstruction

The poor in New Orleans are demanding a democractic reconstruction of their city (Klein, 2005). They are calling for the creation of worker's councils, the formation of neighborhood and local citizen's groups (Schwartz, et al., 2005). They want competitions for the design of public housing, and the full-scale employment of minority contractors and workers in a new Worker's Public Administration program. This will be a *new* New Orleans designed around and embedded in the cultures of those groups the power structure of the city has for too long exploited.

This will be a New Orleans that truly honors black and cajun civic. A democratically reconstructed New Orleans will embrace the disenfranchised, and the poor. Its civic culture will transcend the sadness in that famous blues dirge, "St. James's Infirmary." Stealing and paraphrasing a line from Billie Holliday, "It will be a new day, What a new morning, What a Little Moonlight and some loving civic compassion Can Do!"

* * *

Reality: Expedited Contracts

13 SEPTEMBER, 2005:

> The Army Corps of Engineers will award $1.5 billion in contracts this week for hurricane cleanup operations in Louisiana . . . Just last week, FEMA announced the awarding of several $100 million no-bid contracts . . . Critics noticed that among those receiving contracts were politically connected companies like the Fluor Corporation . . . Halliburton . . . and the Shaw Group . . . which is a client of Joe M. Allbaugh, the former head of FEMA, who now has a private lobbying and consulting firm . . . Halliburton is also a client of Mr. Allbaugh who is a close friend of President Bush (Wayne, 2005, p. C4).

* * *

A racially divided, disorganized, violent, falling-apart-at-the-seams New Orleans; this is George Bush and Karl Rove's gift to America. And as New Orleans rebuilds, crony capitalism rules the day. So much for democratic reconstruction.

Notes

1. Henry Giroux suggested this project. I thank Michael Giardina for his comments on an earlier version.
2. This chronicle of responses to Katriana is confined to the dates of August 29 to 15 September 2005.

References

Alterman, Erioc. (2005, September 26). Found in the Flood. *Nation*, p. 11.

Barry, Dan. (2005, September, 8). Macabre Reminder: The Corpse on Union Street. *New York Times*, pp. A1, A19.

Bush, Barbara. (2005, September 5). Remarks on National Public Radio Marketplace Segment.

Constantine, David, Matthew Ericson and Archie Tse. (2005, September 12). "Neighborhoods That Were Hit Hard and Those That Weren't. *New York Times*, p. A13.

Ford, Richard. (2005, September 4). A City Beyond the Reach of Empathy. *New York Times*, p. Op-Ed, p. 11.

Friedman, Thomas L. (2005, September 7). Osama and Katrina. *New York Times*, Op-Ed., p, A29.

Johnson, Kirk. (2005, September 11). For Storm Survivors, a Mosaic of Impressions Rather Than a Crystalline Moment. *New York Times*, pp. 25, 32.

Klein, Naomi. (2005, September 26). Needed: A People's Reconstruction. *Nation*, p. 12.

Ladson-Billings, Gloria. (2003, April 19). Egon Guba Distinguished Lecture. American Education Research Association Annual Meetings, New Orleans.

Rice, Anne. (2005, September 4). "Do You Know What It Means to Lose New Orleans?" *New York Times*, Op-Ed, p. 11.

Schwartz, John, Andrews Revkin, Matthew Wald, Sewell Chan, Christopere Drew, and Eric Lipton. (2005, September 11). In Trying to Revive New Orleans, Residents Will Face a Challenge of Many Tiers. *New York Times*, pp. A11, A 13.

Wayne, Leslie. (2005, September 13).Expedited Contracts for Cleanup are Testing Regulations. *New York Times*, p. C4.

14

The Secret Downing Street Memo and the Politics of Truth

(12-19-05)

With C. Wright Mills (1959) I believe scholars have an obligation to write their way into their historical moments. The failure to do so makes us complicit with the histories that too often go on behind our backs.

* * *

Published in the *Sunday London Times*, on 1 May 2005, the Downing Street Memo set off a firestorm of controversy. The memo demonstrated that the American and British public had been mislead about the reasons for and the timing of the decision to go to war with Iraq. The secret document indicated that the Bush administration had committed itself to war with Iraq at least a full eight months before the official start of the war which was 19 March 2003. I want to interrogate this history, a history which involves the politics and pragmatics of truth, the manipulation of evidence and facts about the world by governmental officials.

In this interrogation, which is a performance text[1], I move back and forth between local knowledge and global contexts. We are living in dangerous times, year three of the Iraqi War, what Joan Didion and George Orwell call the "New Normal."

SPEAKERS ONE AND TWO: GEORGE ORWELL AND JOAN DIDION (ORWELL, 1984 [1949, PP. 33–45] QUOTED IN DIDION, 2004, P. 71):

> Under the new normal many of us discovered . . . [that] our memories were not satisfactorily under control. We possessed 'pieces of furtive knowledge' that were hard to reconcile with what we heard and read in the news. We saved entire newspapers, hoping that further study might yield their logic, but none emerged (Didion, 2004, p. 71).

The ground upon which we stand has dramatically shifted. We are asked to accept a new set of myths and laws which threaten to destroy what we mean by freedom and democracy. The complex political spaces of the new normal are profoundly shaping the multiple terrains of qualitative inquiry in the 21st Century, including what we mean by words like science, evidence, and truth.

Now the secret memo.

* * *

SPEAKER TWO: DAVID MANNING:

The Secret Downing Street Memo (with some paraphrasing):[2] This is Secret and Strictly Personal—UK Eyes Only.

Iraq: Prime Minister's Meeting, 23 July

This record is extremely sensitive. No further copies should be made. It should be shown only to those with a genuine need to know its contents.

SPEAKER ONE: JOHN SCARLETT

Military action is now seen as inevitable. Bush wants to remove Saddam, through military action, justified by the conjunction of terrorism and WMD.

SPEAKER TWO: C:

The intelligence and facts are being fixed around the policy . . . Bush has made up his mind to take military action . . . The Attorney-General said that the desire for regime change was not a legal case for military action . . . The case (for war) was thin. Saddam was not threatening his neighbors, and his WMD capability was less than that of Libya, North Korea, or Iran.

SPEAKERS ONE AND TWO: TONY BLAIR AND GEORGE W. BUSH:

We stand together on these issues, It is impossible to distinguish between al Qaeda and Saddam (Alterman and Green, 2004, p. 252)

* * *

The memo is chilling. It clearly states that facts and intelligence were being fixed and fitted to conform to a predetermined agenda. Through a series of carefully choreographed presentations involving aerial and ground photographs, statistics, excerpts from secret intelligence memos, Bush and his staff based the case for war on the threats of Saddam's WMDs to the world order (Hersh, 2005, p. 235). They were hesitant, however, to sell the argument for war against Saddam Hussein in August of 2002.

SPEAKER ONE: ANDREW CARD:

> "From a marketing point of view, you don't introduce new products in August" (Rich, 2005c, p. 12).

SPEAKER TWO: BOB WOODWARD:

> Bush initiated plans for the war on November 21, 2001 (Woodward, 2004, p. 1).

But today we know there were no WMD's.[3] There were no links between 9/11 and Saddam. Cheering crowds did not greet American soldiers when they marched into Baghdad.[4]

SPEAKER ONE: FRANK RICH:

> Democracy "was hijacked on the way to war" (Rich, 2005c, p. 12).

* * *

SPEAKER TWO: PRESIDENT BUSH (PRESS CONFERENCE, 4 OCTOBER 2005):

> And we've got to win in Iraq. We will win in Iraq. Iraq's a part of a global war on terror. We're not leaving Iraq.

* * *

Meanwhile, the administration takes to a new level the meaning of the staged news event, borrowing its techniques of news management from Jon Stewart, host of the "Daily Show." Fake newsmen, looking like real newsmen, use the practices of real news programs to deliver fake news in prime time (Rich, 2005a, p. 20).

SPEAKER ONE: FRANK RICH:

> The use of fake reporters—six and counting—producing fake news stories has been exposed. The administration paid $240,000 to Armstrong Williams for delivering faux-journalistic analyses of the No Child Left Behind Act (Rich, 2005b).

Bush's handlers script "town hall" meetings. Under Bush a lie is true if it has the appearance of truth. Manipulating the logic of the lie that looks like the truth insures that Bush's assertions about the real have the appearance of being truthful.

* * *

Truth and Evidence

In times such as this the politics of truth take on increased importance. Many questions are raised. What is truth? What is evidence? What counts as evidence? How is evidence evaluated? How can evidence or facts be "fixed" to fit policy? What kind of evidence-based research should inform this process? How is evidence to be represented? How is evidence to be discounted, or judged to be unreliable or incorrect? What is a fact? What is intelligence? What are the different discourses—law, medicine, history, cultural, or performance studies—that define evidence and truth? (Pring, 2004, p. 203).

SPEAKER TWO: ESTHER KAPLAN AND UNION FOR CONCERNED SCIENTISTS (QUOTED ON KAPLAN, 2005, P. 128):

> There is significant evidence that the scope and scale of the manipulation, suppression, and misrepresentation of science [and evidence] by the Bush administration is unprecedented . . . In the name of pseudo, fake, or junk science, it manufactures evidence to support its positions . . . Indeed, the Bush Administration has taken the concept of evidence to a new level with the endorsement of what is called scientifically based educational research (SBR).
>
> Under the auspices of the 2001 No Child Left Behind Act, the Bush Administration has stated that traditional scientific methods are inadequate for purposes of educational reform. It has endorsed evidence-based models of inquiry, which many regard as inappropriate to human subject research, and nearly impossible to implement in concrete research settings (Ryan and Hood, 2004).
>
> Under the guise of endorsing Intelligent Design, the Administration has launched a full-scale attack on the logic and methods of modern science. Thus, while they have raised the bar concerning the standards for conducting and evaluating educational research, they have similarly moved to debunk these same standards in other areas. This allows them to have it both ways. Modern science cannot get us to where we want to be in our schools, and we will use the methods of science to prove the case!
>
> Drawing from the bio-medical field, SBR emphasizes research practices that produce so-called objective, generalizable evidence (Ryan and Hood, 2004).

Such data, gathered from randomized and non-randomized experimental trials and quantifiable measurement procedures, are used to test causal hypotheses derived from scientific theory. When possible, data are fitted to complex causal models. Evidence based on these assumptions is presumed to be of maximal value for policy makers, practitioners, and the public (Pring, 2004; National Research Council, 2002, p. 47). Evidence that does not conform to these principles is of less value and is not to be encouraged or funded.

There is a great deal at stake in these arguments. As St. Pierre (2004, p. 132) observes, the SBR criteria marginalize many forms of qualitative inquiry, including critical race, queer, postcolonial, feminist, indigenous, and decolonizing theories. The SBR model raises questions that require serious public discussion. The model endorses a narrow view of science and evidence. It celebrates a historical moment when the methods of positivistic science were not being challenged. In valorizing the experimental paradigm, it ignores the many criticisms of experimentalism developed by Donald Campbell over four decades ago, including the inability to adequately treat rival causal factors associated with internal and external validity.

SPEAKER ONE: DONALD CAMPBELL (PARAPHRASE):

The critics of SBR rightfully raise other issues with the paradigm, including its reliance on a naive realism, and its failure to take up the value-fact-theory distinction. The paradigm still acts as if a disinterested observer has a God's eye view of objective reality. It relies on an ethics of deception. It does not address the contexts of knowledge production, nor is it sensitive to the nuances of the researcher-subject relationship (Howe, 2004; Campbell and Stanley, 1963; Lincoln and Guba, 2000).

* * *

These limitations of the SBR model involve the politics of truth. They intersect with the ways in which a given political regime fixes facts and intelligence to fit ideology. What is true, or false, is determined, in part, by the criteria that are used to judge good and bad evidence.

* * *

SBR and the War on truth

There are at least three versions of SBR. SBR One is the model outlined by the National Research Council (2002). SBR Two is a simulacra of SBR One. It was the model used by the Bush administration when it sold the Iraqi war to the world. This model produces simulacra of the truth. SBR Three (below) rejects

SBR One and Two, and articulates a politics and methodology of truth based on a decolonizing critical pedagogy, and a feminist, prophetic ethical pragmatism (Siegfried, 1996; West, 1989, 1991; Denzin, 1996, 2003, 2005).

SBR One, with its focus on objectively verifiable evidence, was not in play when the Bush administration decided to go to war. Instead, they used SBR Two, which allowed them to act as if they were gathering objective, reliable, generalizable evidence. But they were not doing this. The intent, instead, was to gather evidence that appeared to have these characteristics. Under the Bush regime, a fact or piece of evidence is true if it meets three criteria: (a) it has the appearance of being factual; (b) it is patriotic; and (c) it supports a political action that advances the White House's agenda.

Evidence that contradicts that agenda is flawed and biased. The Bush administration wanted to assert its will in the Middle East. It fabricated a set of facts, using their version of SBR One—SBR Two—to justify that activity. Challenges to the war were unpatriotic, and discredited because they undercut the Administration's desire to protect Americans from violent terrorists who oppose our political system.

* * *

The ways in which the world is not a stage are not easy to specify. The dramaturgical politics of the Bush administration is one reason why this is so. Indeed, if, as they demonstrate, everything is already performative, staged, commodified, and dramaturgical, then the dividing line between performer and actor, stage and setting, script and text, performance and reality disappear. As this disappearance occurs, illusion and make-believe prevail. Truthful facts are casualties under such regimes. Misrepresentations are passed off as the truth. When this happens, the right people are not held accountable for the consequences of their actions. The consequences of misrepresentation can be devastating. The likelihood of future catastrophes is increased, and, as in the case of Iraq, people die needlessly (Solomon, 2005, p. B-3).

In this space, where the hyperreal appears more real then the real, pragmatists and cultural critics require apparatuses of resistance and critique, methodologies and pedagogies of truth, ways of making real realities that envision and enact pedagogies of hope. Such pedagogies offer ways of holding fraudulent political regimes accountable for their actions.

* * *

A senior advisor to President Bush (Suskind, 2004, p. 51), described this troubling relationship between performance and reality. He contrasted the so-called "'reality-based community'—people who believe that solutions emerge from . . . judicious study of discernible reality" (p. 51), with his own world view.

SPEAKER ONE: BUSH AIDE:

"That's not the way the world really works anymore. We're an empire now, and when we act, we create our own reality. And while you are studying that reality we'll act again, creating other new realities, which you can study too . . . We're history's actors . . . and you, all of you, will be left to just study what we do" (Suskind, 2004, p. 51).

How do you respond to a statement such as this? Whose history are they creating? And for what ends? Who gave them this power? Who is holding them responsible for the consequences of their historical actions? If they do not like the effects of one reality, they create a new one, to which we must respond, living out the consequences of their experiments in reality construction.

SPEAKER TWO: GEORGE BUSH:

I am praying for strength to do the Lord's will . . . I'm surely not going to justify the war based upon God . . . Nevertheless, in my case, I pray to be as good a messenger of his will as possible (Suskind, 2005, p. 51).

* * *

SBR Three: Critical Pedagogy, Ethics, and Prophetic Pragmatism

Under such circumstances, what does it mean to assert that journalists and social scientists can only write about the realities created by history's actors? What does it mean to state that journalists write the first drafts of history? Whose history, whose reality, and what does reality any longer mean?

When the divisions disappear between reality and its appearances, critical inquiry necessarily becomes disruptive, explicitly pedagogical, and radically democratic. Its topics: fascism, the violent politics of global capitalist culture, the loss of freedom in daily life. We need a new politics of truth. We must embrace the justice of our rage:

SPEAKERS ONE AND TWO: JUNE JORDAN AND PATRICIA HILL COLLINS (PARAPHRASE):

We must reclaim the neglected legacy of the Sixties, an unabashed moral certain-

> ty, an incredible outgoing energy of righteous rage. We cannot restore and expand the forms of justice that our lives require until and unless we change the language of current political and methodological discourse. If we do not reintroduce our concepts of Right and Wrong, of Truth and Evidence, then how shall we finally argue for our cause (Collins, 1998, p. 250; Jordan, 1992, p. 178)?

* * *

I answer the call of Jordan and Collins by turning to the post-pragmatists (see Denzin, 1996 for a review; also Seigfried, 1996). For the post-pragmatist feminist there is no neutral standpoint, no objective God's eye view of the world. The meaning of a concept, or line of action, or a representation lies in the practical, political, moral, and social consequences it produces for an actor or collectivity. The meanings of these consequences are not objectively given. They are established through social interaction and the politics of representation. All representations are historically situated, shaped by the intersecting contingencies of power, gender, race and class (Siegfried, 1996, p. 269; Collins, 2000).

An Afro-Centric, feminist ethical framework (Collins, 2000; 1998) mediates the pragmatic theory of meaning. Collins (2000) offers four criteria—primacy of lived experience, dialogue, an ethics of care, an ethics of responsibility—for interpreting truth and knowledge claims. This framework privileges lived experience, emotion, empathy, and values rooted in personal expressiveness (Collins, 2000, pp. 265–269; Edwards and Mauthner, 2002, p. 25).

The moral inquirer, whether a politician or a social scientist, builds a collaborative, reciprocal, trusting, mutually accountable relationship with those studied. This feminist ethical framework is care- and justice-based. It seeks to contextualize shared values and norms. It privileges the sacredness of life, human dignity, nonviolence, care, solidarity, love, community, empowerment, civic transformation. It demands of any action that it positively contribute to a politics of resistance, hope, and freedom (Denzin, 2003, p. 258).

For the prophetic post-pragmatists there are no absolute truths, no absolute principles, no faith-based beliefs in what is true or false. Following Collins (2000), Pelias (2004, p. 163), and Freire (1999), the moral inquirer enacts a politics of love and care, an ethic of hope and forgiveness.

SPEAKER ONE: RON PELIAS (PARAPHRASE):

> The heart learns that stories are truths that won't keep still. The heart learns that facts are the possibilities we pretend we trust. The heart's method of pumping, loving, and forgiving encourages us to proceed with our hearts first. What matters

> most is that we learn how to use our rage in positive ways, to love, to struggle, to forgive. We have little other choice (Pelias, 2004, pp. 162–163, 171).

In a methodology of the heart, actions are judged in terms of moral consequences and the meanings people bring to them. Consequences are not self-evident. They are socially constructed. The concept of truth is thus replaced with a consequential theory of meaning. Experience, folded through what Stuart Hall (1996, p. 473) calls the politics of representation, becomes the site of meaning and truth. Facts about the world are treated as facticities, as lived experiences. The pragmatist examines the effects, or consequences, of any line of action on existing structures of domination. The pragmatist asks, that is, what are the moral and ethical consequences of these effects for lived human experience. If people are being oppressed, denied freedom, or dying because of these effects, then the action, of course, is morally indefensible.

SPEAKER TWO. CORNEL WEST (1991, P. 36; 1989, P. 234; PARAPHRASED):

> At the level of politics and ideology, the post-pragmatist acts as a critical moral agent, one whose political goal is the creation of greater individual freedom in the broader social order. Prophetic pragmatists as moral agents understand that the consequences of their interventions into the world are exclusively political, judged always in terms of their contributions to a politics of liberation, love, caring, and freedom.

* * *

The processes that shape national security decision-making in a democracy should be transparent and open. They should not be based, as were the Bush Administration's decisions to go to war, on cherry-picked intelligence, disinformation, secrecy, secret information, secrets that are not secrets, leaked, declassified and reclassified documents, coded phrases, misrepresentations, distortions, and lies (Sanger, 2005, pp. 1, 5). Evidence should not be doctored (Rich, 2005d, p. 13). Contradictory evidence should be openly discussed, its implications for policy debated. Decisions "should be subjected to a robust process of checks and balance" (Herbert, 2005. p. A23).

* * *

Leading scientists, including more than 60 Nobel Prize winners, have all spoken out against these abuses of science under the Bush regime (Kaplan, 2005, pp. 95, 104, 113). The hallmark of a free society is its unfettered support of research and inquiry on ethically and politically sensitive, controversial issues.

Such research yields trustworthy findings that many, including those in political power, may find objectionable. But a society's respect for critical interpretive inquiry is "based on the common understanding that serious health, economic, and social consequences are at stake" (Hillman, 2003).

Safe guards protecting scientists and the scientific community from censorship, misrepresentation, repression and politicization must be commonplace. The values of progressive democracy must be forefront when scientific advice is used for policymaking decisions. The pragmatic consequences for a radical democracy must be taken into account when scientific recommendations for social action are implemented. It is time for all concerned scholars and citizens to rally against the misuses of science, information, and evidence by the Bush administration (Mooney, 2005, p. 255).

* * *

Back To Downing Street And History's Actors

The morally unethical actions of Bush and his administration are exposed in the Downing Street memo. Like the high level leaks that unmasked whistleblower Joseph Wilson's wife Valerie as a covert C. I. A. agent, the memo shows that Bush's History's Actors, or the White House Iraq Group (WHIG) as they called themselves, were willing to go to any length to justify the war in Iraq. They took the concept of truth as a social construction to a logical but ethically indefensible conclusion. In so doing they exposed the vulnerability of an epistemology and methodology that relies upon manipulations of the world to produce findings that conform to one's beliefs about reality. Thus did WHIG discredit SBR One, showing that it has no full-proof mechanism for producing objective truth.

As long as reality can be socially constructed, fraudulent versions of SBR One, what I have called SBR Two, will be created. In that space history's actors must be held accountable to a higher moral truth. A methodology of the heart, a prophetic, feminist post-pragmatism embraces an ethics of truth grounded in love, care, hope, and forgiveness.

SPEAKER ONE: PATRICIA HILL COLLINS (2000, P. 251, PARAPHRASE):

> This methodology relies on a righteous rage to spur us on, to keep us headed in the right direction, to point the way, to move people toward justice. If it does this, then it has made a very important difference in the lives of people.

* * *

We demand that history's actors use models of evidence that answer to these moral truths.

Notes

1. The text is to be performed on a stage with three speakers: a narrator at a podium and speakers A and B seated behind a table. Speakers A and B assume the voices of a variety of persons, including Joan Didion, President Bush, Tony Blair, and George Orwell. A spotlight moves to each speaker when it is his or her turn to speak. When speaking, the speaker first announces the name of the person being spoken for.
2. The text reads:
   This is Secret and Strictly Personal—UK Eyes Only
   David Manning
   FR: Matthew Rycroft
   Date: 23 July 2002
   cc: Defence Secretary, Foreign Secretary, Attorney-General, Sir Richard Wilson, John Scarlett, Francis Richards, CDS, C. Jonathan Powell, Sally Morgan, Alastair Campbell
   IRAQ: PRIME MINISTER'S MEETING, 23 JULY
   This record is extremely sensitive. No further copies should be made. It should be shown only to those with a genuine need to know its contents.
   John Scarlett summarised the intelligence and latest JIC assessment . . . C reported on his recent talks in Washington . . . Military action was now seen as inevitable. Bush wanted to remove Saddam, through military action, justified by the conjunction of terrorism and WMD. But the intelligence and facts were being fixed around the policy . . . It seemed clear that Bush had made up his mind to take military action . . . The Attorney-General said that the desire for regime change was not a legal case for military action . . . But the case (for war) was thin. Saddam was not threatening his neighbors, and his WMD capability was less than that of Libya, North Korea, or Iran.
3. Since no WMDs were found, the reasons for the war had to be changed. They now include bringing American-style democracy to Iraq and the Middle East; fighting terrorists in Iraq before they strike America; and honoring the dead who have been killed in the war.
4. Saddam did not represent a threat to America, nor to the world. There were no secret purchases of uranium oxide from the African nation of Niger (Alterman and Green, 2004, p. 265). No one will take responsibility for, nor be accountable for, the mass destruction, the murders, and the violence that have occurred since the beginning of the war. Facts: over 2000 dead American soldiers; more than 30,000 dead Iraqi; disgrace and degradation in Abu Ghraib.

References

Alterman, Eric and Mark Green. (2004). *The Book on Bush: How George W. (Mis)Leads America.* New York: Penguin.

Campbell, Donald and Julian C. Stanley. (1963). *Experimental and Quasi-Experimental Designs.* Chicago: Rand McNally.

Collins, Patricia Hill. (1998). *Fighting Words: Black Women & the Search for Justice.* Minneapolis: University of Minnesota Press.

Collins, Patricia Hill. (2000). *Black Feminist Thought*, 2/e. New York: Routledge.

Denzin, Norman K. (2005). "Emancipatory Discourses and the Ethics and Politics of Interpretation." In N. K. Denzin and Y.S. Lincoln (eds.), *Handbook of Qualitative Research*, 3/e, pp. 933–958. Thousand Oaks: Sage.

Denzin, Norman K. (2003). *Performance Ethnography: Critical Pedagogy and the Politics of Culture.* Thousand Oaks: Sage.

Denzin, Norman K. (1996). "Post-Pragmatism." *Symbolic Interaction*, 19 (1), pp. 61–75.

Didion, Joan. (2004, October 21). Politics in the 'New Normal' America. *New York Review of Books*, 51, (16), pp. 64–73.

Edwards, Rosalind and Melanie Mauthner. (2002). Ethics and Feminist Research: Theory and Practice. In Melanie Mauthner, Maxine Birch, Julie Jessop and Tina Miller (Eds.), *Ethics in Qualitative Research*, pp. 14–31. London: Sage.

Freire, Paulo. (1999). *Pedagogy of Hope*, translated by Robert R. Barr. New York: Continuum. (Originally published 1992).

Hall, Stuart. (1996) What Is This 'Black' in Black Popular Culture? In David Morley and Kuan-Hsing Chen (Eds.), *Stuart Hall: Critical Dialogues in Cultural Studies*, pp. 465–475. London: Routledge.

Herbert, Bob. (2005, October 20). "How Scary Is This?" " *New York Times*, Op-Ed, p. A23.

Hersh, Seymour M. (2005). *Chain of Command: The Road from 9/11 to Abu Ghraib.* New York: HarperCollins.

Hillman, Sally T. (2003, November 3). NIH Funded Research and the Peer-Review Process. American Sociological Association Press Release.

Howe, Kenneth R. (2004). A Critique of Experimentalism. *Qualitative Inquiry*, 10, pp. 42–61.

Jordan, June. (1992). *Technical Difficulties: African-American Notes on the State of the Union.* New York: Pantheon.

Kaplan, Esther. (2005). *With God on Their Side: George W. Bush and the Christian Right.* New York: The New Press.

Lincoln, Yvonna S. and Egon G. Guba. (2000). Paradigmatic Controversies, Contradictions, and Emerging Confluences. In N. K. Denzin and Y. S. Lincoln (Eds.). *Handbook of Qualitative Research, 2/e*, pp. 163–188. Thousand Oaks: Sage.

Mills, C. Wright. (1959). *The Sociological Imagination.* New York: Oxford.

Mooney, Chris. (2005). *The Republican War on Science.* New York: Basic Books.

National Research Council. (2002). *Scientific Research in Education*. Washington, D.C.: National Academy Press.

New York Times. (2005, October 4). Editorial Page. Faux News Is Bad News, p. A-28.

Orwell, George. (1949). *Nineteen Eighty-Four*. New York: Harcourt, Brace and Company.

Pelias, R. J. (2004). *A methodology if the heart: evoking academic and daily life* (Walnut Creek, CA, AltaMira).

Pring, Richard. (2004). Conclusion: Evidence-based Policy and Practice. In Gary Thomas and Richard Pring (Eds.). *Evidence-Based Practice in Education*, pp. 201–212. New York: Open University Press.

Rich, Frank. (2005a, February 20). The White House Stages Its 'Daily Show.' *New York Times*, Arts & Leisure, Section 2, pp. 1, 20.

Rich, Frank. (2005b, March 20). "Enron: Patron Saint of Bush's Fake News."' *New York Times*, Arts & Leisure, Section 2, pp. 1, 8.

Rich, Frank. (2005c, October 16). It's Bush-Cheney, Not Rove-Libby. *New York Times*, Op-Ed, Op-Ed, p. 12.

Rich, Frank. (2005d, October 23). Karl and Scooter's Excellent Adventure. *New York Times*, Op-Ed, Op-Ed, p. 13.

Ryan, Katherine and Lisa Hood. (2004). Guarding the Castle and Opening the Gates. *Qualitative Inquiry*, 10, pp. 79–95.

Seigfried, Charlene Haddock. (1996). *Pragmatism and Feminism: Reweaving the Social Fabric*. Chicago: University of Chicago Press.

Solomon, John. (2005, September 15). Truth Watch: Failed Levees Had Already Been Fortified. *The News Gazette*, p. B-3.

Suskind, R. (2004). Faith, certainty, and the presidency of George W., *New York Times Magazine*, 17 October, Section 6, pp. 44–51, 64, 102, 106.

St. Pierre, Elizabeth A. (2004). Refusing Alternatives: A Science of Contestation. *Qualitative Inquiry*, 10, pp. 130–139.

Suskind, R. (2004, October 17). Faith, Certainty, and the Presidency of George W. Bush. *The New York Times Magazine*, Section 6, pp. 44–51, 64, 102, 106.

West, Cornel. (1991). Theory, Pragmatisms and Politics. In Jonathan Arac and Barbara Johnson (Eds.), *Consequences of Theory*, pp. 22–38. Baltimore: Johns Hopkins University Press.

West, Cornel. (1989). *The American Evasion of Philosophy: A Genealogy of Pragmatism*. Madison: University of Wisconsin Press.

Woodward, Bob. (2004). *Plan of Attack*. New York: Simon and Schuster.

15

Six Years of Magical Thinking

GEORGE BUSH:

> You know. . . . I'm basically a media creation. I've never done anything. I've worked for my dad. I've worked in the oil business. But that's not the kind of profile you have to have to get elected to public office (Bush quoted in Reed, 1989; also in Lindorff and Olshansky, 2006, p. 20).)

GEORGE BUSH:

> My vision is clear, but, hey, we took a thumpin'.

* * *

Dateline: 5 November 2006, Dick Cheney, ABC Sunday morning News,
DICK CHENEY:

> President Bush will not change U. S. policy in Irag, even if the Republicans lose control of the House and the Senate. "There might be some effect in Congress. But the attitude in the White House is 'full speed ahead.' We're not running for office. We're doing what we think is right" (Cheney, in Stolberg and Sanger, 2006, p. A 18).

The Vice-President might have said, quoting, Joan Didion (2001, p. 12) that,

> In a democracy such as ours, voting is merely a consumer transaction. We packaged and sold the war on terror as a way of winning the 2004 election.

The President would agree.

GEORGE BUSH (COMMENTING ON THE 2004 PRESIDENTIAL ELECTION):

> "Let me put it to you this way. I earned capital in the campaign, political capital, and now I intend to spend it" (Bush, in Stolberg and Sanger, 2006, p. A 18).

* * *

Bush Foreign policy. You can spell it with seven letters: I R A Q W AR. You CAN SCRAMBLE the letters, turn them around: RAW WAR. Make different words: IRAQWAR, WARIRAQ, IRAQRAW, RAWIRAQ. Add the letters BUSH and CHENEY to the mix: IRAGBUSHCHENEYWAR; CHENEYWAR; CHENEYRAWWAR. You can go crazy doing this.

* * *

This is year four of the Iraqi War, longer now than World War II. We are living under what Joan Didion and George Orwell call the "New Normal" (Orwell, [1949, pp. 33–45] quoted in Didion, 2004, p. 71) Under the new normal, nothing any longer made sense. Why did we go to war? The fact that there were no WMDs no longer mattered. We went to war because God spoke to Bush. How do we know God spoke to Bush? We have to take this on faith, but whose faith? Under the New Normal life turned into a never-ending nightmare, a lost week-end that started after the stolen election in 2000. When will this painful nightmare end? What will they do next? What have they done? Does it any longer matter?

Who could believe that they were doing what they were doing: a gulag of outsourced torture camps, wiretaps, abuse at Abu Ghraib, truthiness and faux news stories, missing WMDs, anthrax scares, Orange Alerts, war profiteering, tax cuts for the rich, cuts in support for education and health care, environmental destruction, global warming, Katrina, Patriot Acts, detainees, faith-based government, faith-based science, faith-based social services, faith-based justice, faith-based health care, faith-based wars (Wills, 2006), Guantanamo, false V-1 days, Karl Rove, Karen Hughes, Jack Abramoff, Secret Downing Street memos, Swift Boaters, embedded reporters, Fox News, media control, 9/11 commissions, No Child Left Behind, Axis of Evil, Pat Tillman, war on terror, terrorism and the politics of fear (Altheide, 2006), war without-end anthraxwmd,orangeglobalalertfaithbasedRove.

* * *

Joan Didion called it the year of magical thinking, 2003–2004, the year her husband, John Gregory Dunne, and daughter Quintana died. Magical thinking, looking for patterns where there were none, making meaning by putting disconnected events together, finding meaning in furtive memories, stubbornly holding on to the past: not wanting to give away or move John's shoes because he would need them when he returned (Didion, 2005, p. 37). Insisting on being alone the night John died so that he could come back. Wrapping Christmas presents with John's favorite paper, putting up Christmas lights around John's reading chair. On the surface Didion appeared normal, rational, yet underneath she lived in chaos, her life was out of control. She lost the skills for ordinary social interaction. She did not have the resilience she had a year earlier. She feared she would die, "If the telephone rang when I was in the shower I no longer answered it, to avoid falling to death on the tile" (2005, p. 47).

Magical thinking, being incapable of rational thought, but trying to appear normal, using magic to hold things together. If she thought something, or made a connection between two things, then in fact the two things were connected—faking being normal. The year of magical thinking, the year of being normal and crazy at the same time.

* * *

It has been six years of magical, wishful thinking under George W. Bush. Normal crazy, life as cognitive chaos. We howled at the moon, lost our patience, embraced apathy, gave up, turned our backs on the world. A new form of crazy—bushwacked crazy! (Ivins, 2003).

Many of us developed anti-Bush rituals—ways to ward off apathy, insanity, and the evil empire. Not watching a Bush speech on C-Span meant he had not given that speech. Some thought that if they saved entire newspapers and clipped Bush stories that a hidden logic would be revealed. They would prove that Bush was evil, that he lied, misrepresented, favored the rich, was racist, that he was fascist, an elitist, arrogant, mean-spirited, insecure, not well informed, lived in a bubble, butchered the English language, obsessed about exercising and his weight and was dumb.

* * *

Like Didion, I made fragile links between seemingly disconnected events, finding meanings everywhere. For example, the Bush family friendship with Billy Graham could be used to explaine the President's support of big business.

This friendship explained his support of the religious right. In turn, his born-again Christianity explained his support of the neo-conservatives, his opposition to stem-cell research and his belief that global warming is not happening. In short, a single event caused a complex chain of other events to occur. There was an effort to get behind the evil to its underlying cause or causes.

* * *

We forgot these lines **from George:** "You know. . . . I'm basically a media creation." We needed to look no further. As a media creation and a member of America's ruling class, Bush always acted in the best interests of his social class. Underlying, background causal variables like religion, Billy Graham, neo-conservative ideology, big business, and the media were and are all part of the same social construction. His social class won, our social class lost. End of story.

* * *

But we persisted. We gave money to anti-war causes, put anti-war signs in our front yards, renewed our subscriptions to left and progressive magazines, read British, French, and German newspapers. We read Bush family biographies. We established Bush family links to the Nazis in WWII. We scoured the Internet for new stories that discredited him. We collected books that proved he lied. We made fun of his speeches, his intelligence, somebody said Karl Rove was Bush's brain. Molly Ivins and Lou Dubose (2003), said we were 'Bushwacked", blind-sided, made fools of. If people had only paid attention, this man had a horrendous record as governor of Texas.

Investigative journalists, reporters, columnists, sociologists, social theorists, and critics got into the act: Alterman, Altheide, Corn, Danner, Dowd, Franken, Giroux, Glantz, Gordon, Green, Habermas, Hersh, Isikoff, Kaplan, Keillor, Kellner, Krugman,Lindoroff and Olshansky, Matthews, Moody, Moore, Raban, Rich, Ricks, Risen, Suskind, Risen, Trainor, Trillin, Woodward. Book after book documented the destruction, misrepresentation, abuses of power, and the scandals of this administration.

There was no shortage of readers for these books and these narratives; many became best sellers. The problem was not changing people's consciousness, or finding people who agreed with the criticisms. The problem was changing the regimes that produced the truths in the first place (Foucault, 1980, p. 133).

* * *

Life Under Bush: A Three-Act Play

Like others, I imposed a narrative structure, created a story-line for a new three, or was it four, act play called "The New Normal, or Life Under Bush." **Act One,** "The Stolen Election" has three major scenes: the extra 36 days until the Supreme Court awarded the election to Bush; the tax cuts, and the No Child Left Behind Act. Act One ends with the 9/11/01 attacks and the decision to go to war in Afghanistan.

Act Two, "Going to War" has four major scenes: Saddam, or the lies about Saddam leading up to the invasion of Iraq; WMDS—where did they go?; War Scandals, including the war on terror, Abu Ghraib, the government domestic spying campaign and the violation of civil liberties; Civil War, or the collapse of civil society in Iraq.

We are in the first scene of **Act Three,** "We Took a Thumpin". In this act the voters "strip the president and his party of control of the House and the Senate and install Democratic majorities in the Capitol" (Broder, 2006). In scene two, New Power, the democrats take power, debate when and how to get out of Iraq, while Bush sulks, fires Rumsfeld, and waits for the Iraqi War report from the Baker Committee. Scenes three and four have yet to be written. Currently scene three extends through the 2008 presidential primaries and election cycle, and the departure of Bush from the White House. In scene four (We Won) Bush and the new president both take credit for victory in Iraq and the formal withdrawal of Americans troops from that war-torn nation.

* * *

Truth to Power, Truth to Experience

Following Foucault (1980), and other good progressives who believe in the power of words and the power of the press, in confronting the Bush Regime we believed we were speaking truth to power and truth to experience. We believed that if the lies were uncovered, then the truth of experience under Bush would prevail. This was another version of magical thinking. We believed that insider stories about Rove and the Bush Dynasty would force the truth to be told and bring down the walls of power. We only needed to buy the latest book to prove our case. We put a hold on Woodward's (2006) *State of Denial*. We turned page after page, looking for those fart stories that Rove and Bush told each other. And nothing happened. Until November 7 2006.

* * *

George: "We took a thumpin'"

* * *

And they did take a thumpin! The clamor of voices heard at the ballot boxes across America said that "enough is enough." The voters said the emperor has no clothes, we know he lies. We want him out of power! The voters spoke from the site of personal experience. They spoke truth to experience. They spoke about slain daughters and sons in Iraq, unemployment, disappearing retirement funds, foreclosures on homes, broken down hospitals and schools. They spoke, they voted. Barebones, ballot-box democracy prevailed, not that top-down kind of democracy Bush tried to install in Iraq.

Any Winners?

So who won? The Republicans are out and the Democrats are back in. The war goes on. Scene Three, Act Three is not over. The super-rich are richer than ever, if that is even possible. The death toll in Iraq is unfathomable—hundreds of thousands have died, nearly 3,000 Americans at last count.

Underneath, those who were in power, remain in power. But the strategies remain the same. We need our myths and our rituals, we need magical thinking, in all its forms. We need a never-ending stream of counter-hegemonic discourse. Without these cognitive and emotional structures we would not be able to go on, to resist. We need to to expose the lies and the injustices that are committed by those in power. Those in power must have their feet held to the fire, held accountable for their actions.

We cannot allow statements like the following:

DICK CHENEY (ON IRAN):

> The lack of evidence concerning Iran's smoking nuclear power means they have it (Cheney in Hersh, 2006, p. 102).

DICK CHENEY (ON INDULGENT, LAZY JOURNALISTS):

> The press is, with all due respect . . . oftentimes lazy (Cheney quoted in Kristof, 2006, p, A25).

PAUL WOLFOWITZ (ON JOURNALISTS AS COWARDS):

> Part of our problem is a lot of the press are afraid to travel . . . so they sit in Baghdad and they publish rumors (Wolfowitz quoted in Kristof, 2006, p, A25).

DON RUMSFELD (ON TREASON AND THE JOURNALISTS):

> All of the exaggerations seem to be on one side. It isn't as though there have been a series of random errors on both sides of issues. On the contrary, the steady stream of errors all seems to be of a nature to inflame the situation and to give heart to the terrorists and to discourage those who hope for success in Iraq (Rumsfeld quoted in Kristof, 2006, p, A25).

Thus do those in power attempt to subvert the truths that journalists (and others) write about the war in Iraq. Truth, Foucault reminds us, must contest, and be freed from official representations of reality. We cannot allow the statements of Bush, Cheney, Rumsfeld and Wolfowitz to go unchallenged.

Forms of resistance must be staged, including sit-ins (Cindy Sheehan), war protests, political theatre, and ethnodramas which unravel the cruel truths of the war (Riding. 2004). Such works, using interviews, and published documents, re-enact the views of Bush and others in his administration, exposing the contradictions and lies that are contained in their public performances. These works speak truth to experience. They enact pedagogies of resistance, much like the political theatre that occurred when Americans on 7 November 2006 went into voting booths, and told George W. Bush that he had used up all his political capital. It was time, the voters said, to give DUBYA a good old fashioned, down-home thumpin'!

References

Altheide, Dav id L. (2006). *Terrorism and the Politics of Fear*. Lanham, MD: AltaMira Press.

Broder, David. (2006, November 20). After Vote, Bush's Status Drops into Weak Position. *News-Gazette*, p. A-8.

Didion, Joan. (2006). *We Tell Ourselves Stories In Order To Live: Collected Nonfiction*. New York: Everyman's Library.

Didion, Joan. (2005). *The Year of Magical Thinking*. New York: Alfred Knopf.

Didion, Joan. (2004, October 21). Politics in the 'New Normal' America. *New York Review of Books*, 51, (16), pp. 64 73.

Didion, Joan. (2001). *Political Fictions*. New York: Vintage.

Foucault, Michel., (1980). *Power/Knowledge: Selected Interviews & Other Writings, 1972–1977*. Edited by Colin Gordon. New York: Pantheon Books.

Foucault, Michel. (2000). *Essential Works of Foucault: 1954–1984, Volume Three, Power*. Edited by James D. Fabion, New York: Free Press.

Freire, Paulo. (2001). *Pedagogy of the Oppressed*, 30th Anniversary Edition, New York: Continuum.

Hersh, Seymour. (2006, November 27). Annals of National Security: The Next Act: A Damaged White House eyes Iran. *The New Yorker*, pp. 94–107.

Ivins, Molly, and Lou Dubose. (2003). *Bushwacked: Life in George W. Bush's America.* New York: Random House.

Kristof, Nicholas D. (2006, November 28). The Cowards Turned Out to Be Right. *New York Times*, Op-Ed, p. A25.

Lindorff, Dave, and Barbara Olshansky. (2006). *The Case for Impeachment: The Legal Argument for Removing President George W. Bush from Office.* New York: Thomas Dunne Books, St. Martin's Press.

Orwell, George. (1949). *Nineteen Eighty-Four.* New York: Harcourt, Brace and Company.

Reed, Steven R. (1989, July 2). President Bush's Son on a Roll/Important Decisions Ahead for George W. *Houston Chronicle*, p. 3.

Riding, A. (2004, June 15). On a London Stage: A Hearing For Guantanamo Detainees. *New York Times*, p. B2.

Stolberg, Sheryl Gay, and David E. Sanger. (2006, November 6). Win, Lose or Draw, Bush Faces Unfamiliar Terrain. *New York Times*, (National), p. A-18.

Wills, Gary. (2006, November 16) . A Country Ruled by Faith. *New York Review of Books*, 53, (18), pp. 8–12.

Woodward, Bob. (2006). *State of Denial: Bush at War, Part III.* New York: Simon and Schuster.

Index

A

B

E

F

G

H

I

J

K

L

M

N

O

P

R

S

T

U

V

W

Studies in the Postmodern Theory of Education

General Editors
Joe L. Kincheloe & Shirley R. Steinberg

Counterpoints publishes the most compelling and imaginative books being written in education today. Grounded on the theoretical advances in criticalism, feminism, and postmodernism in the last two decades of the twentieth century, Counterpoints engages the meaning of these innovations in various forms of educational expression. Committed to the proposition that theoretical literature should be accessible to a variety of audiences, the series insists that its authors avoid esoteric and jargonistic languages that transform educational scholarship into an elite discourse for the initiated. Scholarly work matters only to the degree it affects consciousness and practice at multiple sites. Counterpoints' editorial policy is based on these principles and the ability of scholars to break new ground, to open new conversations, to go where educators have never gone before.

For additional information about this series or for the submission of manuscripts, please contact:

Joe L. Kincheloe & Shirley R. Steinberg
c/o Peter Lang Publishing, Inc.
29 Broadway, 18th floor
New York, New York 10006

To order other books in this series, please contact our Customer Service Department:

(800) 770-LANG (within the U.S.)
(212) 647-7706 (outside the U.S.)
(212) 647-7707 FAX

Or browse online by series:

www.peterlang.com

Zeitfracht Medien GmbH
Ferdinand-Jühlke-Straße 7
99095 Erfurt, Deutschland
produktsicherheit@kolibri360.de

Druck:
CPI Druckdienstleistungen GmbH
im Auftrag der
Zeitfracht Medien GmbH
Ein Unternehmen der Zeitfracht - Gruppe
Ferdinand-Jühlke-Str. 7
99095 Erfurt